Journaling Through:

Unleashing the Power of the Authentic Self

D1529820

bright sky press
HOUSTON, TEXAS

2365 Rice Blvd., Suite 202 Houston, Texas 77005

ISBN 978-1-933979-58-8

10   9   8   7   6   5   4   3   2   1

Library of Congress information on file with publisher.

Edited by Hillary Durgin Harmon
Printed in the United States of America

Journaling Through:
Unleashing the Power of the Authentic Self

**Seven Benefits of
Unlocking the
Wisdom Within**

ANGELA CAUGHLIN

bright sky press
HOUSTON, TEXAS

To my many teachers along the Path

Table of *Contents*

Introduction

Part One: *The Divine Gift*

Part Two: *The Seven Benefits: How Journaling Unlocks the Wisdom Within*

Part Three: Journaling Through: At Work

Part Four: Tools for Transforming Your Life

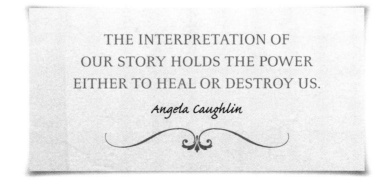

THE INTERPRETATION OF
OUR STORY HOLDS THE POWER
EITHER TO HEAL OR DESTROY US.

Angela Caughlin

Introduction

My relationship with journaling started with an unexpected change in my own path, many years ago. I began to journal out of sheer desperation, reeling from the shock of the death of my young husband, knowing somewhere deep in my bones that journaling was my salvation.

I did not understand why journaling seemed to work so well but realized that after journaling, I felt clear and had a new perspective, with added focus and energy. I could write things I could not say out loud or to anyone else. As with any close relationship, sometimes I despised journaling, and sometimes it was my best friend, but I always knew I could count on it—journaling worked. Through my own experience as a psychotherapist and observing the journaling experiences of many others throughout the years, it became clear to me that journaling offered a way to chip away at the blocks, emotions, and beliefs that hold us captive, unleashing the thoughts that lie buried deep within each of us.

My lessons in journaling continued and beckoned me to help others experiment with journaling as a natural movement forward with powerful results. Although my experiences with journaling implied that it was an integral part of the healing and transformative experience, it was not until a few years ago that I was able to begin to piece together all of the reasons and information about exactly why journaling works so well.

Never before has so much information been available to assist us to understand the magnificent connections between the brain, body, and spiritual realm. It is this new field of research that gives credibility to what, until now, was unrecognized or considered merely a theory. These links allow us to understand how journaling can access the mind/body/spirit connections that work together to help us change and understand our own story. I have found the why of journaling, the reason it really helps us to awaken, and I want to share that discovery with you.

We have approximately sixty thousand thoughts a day that go through our minds, most of which are repetitious. We have a thinking body. Thoughts are not only contained in our mind but are carried throughout our cellular being by the chemicals they create. Every thought creates a chemical. As our sensory system responds to certain memories over and over, we reinterpret ourselves according to those memories, recreating the chemical response as well. Writing helps us avoid repetition.

I have identified seven clear benefits of journaling—health, awareness, connection, focus, creativity, authenticity, and vision and dreams. As we explore the exercises and questions associated with each benefit, our writing clears old thoughts, allowing for new thoughts to bubble up. History is no longer repeating itself!

Change, the theme that is riveting through our culture today, should be viewed as a positive, a welcome, fresh new energy, being released into the cosmos as we journal. But we cannot make changes without knowing what we need to change. This means asking the right questions to uncover the thoughts that reside within us. So, before we can decide what we need to change, we have to rediscover who we are and understand our own story.

Using journaling as your tool, this workbook is for anyone who is interested in creating a more authentic and effective life. The exercises are designed to help you generate new thoughts, ideas, and solutions, and to align them with your true purpose and authentic self. This workbook gives you the opportunity to explore new ways to navigate change as you discover the power inside yourself.

In my practice as a psychotherapist and coach, I have always believed that each individual possesses the answers to his or her questions within. My job is to help guide a person through the right questions in order to gain a new perspective and to find the answers that are waiting to be discovered, the "Aha." I know that when the right questions resonate, the answers will appear.

For years, I have written down questions to help individuals journal, or used exercises in workshops to dig deeper to find their own answers to clear "old tapes." After numerous requests, I have introduced my "Seven Benefits of Journaling" along with the exercises and questions I have used in my workshops, and combined them into one workbook, one for professional use and one for personal use.

GO CONFIDENTLY IN THE
DIRECTION OF YOUR DREAMS.
ACT AS THOUGH IT WERE
IMPOSSIBLE TO FAIL.
Dorothea Brandt

As we journal to discover our innermost thoughts and feelings, we become the observer of our own path, heightening the awareness of our values, behaviors, beliefs, experiences, and subtle movements in our own consciousness. As we clear out old, stuck programs and beliefs, we have the unique opportunity to see the world with fresh eyes as we realize we can participate in the creation of our journey. A conscious commitment to participate in our own journey gives us a sense of freedom and accomplishment, grounding us in the direction we are choosing to follow.

In identifying the Seven Benefits of Journaling, I have attempted to answer the question of why people should journal. As you begin to review the exercises associated with each of the Seven Benefits, I hope you will allow new thoughts to cascade through your mind like tiny bubbles, using them as an inspirational tool to unlock the information stored deep inside of you.

Journaling can extend our story beyond our own mind and spin it into the context of the world. Writing and journaling challenge us to search our soul and our story for meaning, capturing the moments along the way. In the book *Man's Search for Meaning*, Viktor Frankl says, "What matters, therefore, is not the meaning of life in general but rather the specific meaning of a person's life at a given moment."[1] Journaling helps us distill these moments into something that can help us to grow.

I invite you to join me in journaling. It is my intention that through this workbook, you will experience the power of the process of journaling. As your story unfolds, listen to the messages it brings forth. Allow your body, mind, and spirit to heal as you record old memories and perhaps let them go. Remember, journaling is a process; it doesn't happen all at once. As we let go of the past, we can give our attention to the present and begin to unleash the reserves of creative energy that help restore and transform our lives. Allow your consciousness to expand as journaling guides you toward the realm of the possible.

So ... Before We Journal ...
We have an experience
A thought is bubbling up
the thought triggers a belief
that is usually unconscious
which is triggering other, old thoughts and beliefs
which continues to take us around the loop of the subconscious
repeating the same thoughts
releasing the same chemicals to our cells
repeating the same actions
reinforcing the same values or "learned truths"
as we connect with the field that magnetically
brings us what we believe ...
is our story ... that we continue to live out of ... again and again

----

And After We Journal ...
We are dissecting our experiences, looking at them in a new way,
allowing us to let go of old thoughts from the subconscious
which changes our perception of a situation,
and triggers new thoughts from the conscious
releasing new chemicals to our cells
which when repeated over and over
create new neurons that are firing together with other neurons
as our thoughts create sharp pictures in our minds,
which are creating new neural pathways
which are changing our beliefs
allowing us to change our actions
and reexperience life in a new way
reinforcing new values or "truths"
which connect with the electromagnetic fields within us and outside of us ...
which brings us exactly what we believe
that changes our story
and our destiny forever ... and ever ...

Angela Caughlin

PART ONE

The
Divine Gift

The Practice of Journaling

Where Did Journaling Begin?

*T*HROUGHOUT THE EVOLUTION OF WRITING, MAN HAS FELT IT WAS HIS GIFT TO BE ABLE TO RECORD HIS OWN STORY, WHETHER IN PICTURES, ON CLAY, OR ON PARCHMENT. ACCORDING TO HISTORIANS, THE FIRST PICTURES WERE CAVE PAINTINGS MADE ALMOST TWENTY-TWO THOUSAND YEARS AGO. IT WOULD BE ANOTHER SEVENTEEN MILLENNIA BEFORE HUMANS ACTUALLY BEGAN THE ART OF WRITING. HIEROGLYPHS TOLD THE STORIES OF CIVILIZATIONS AND RECORDED THE EVENTS THAT HAPPENED IN FAMILIES AND CULTURES. WRITING WAS BORN OUT OF NECESSITY AS RELIABLE ORAL RECORDS COULD NOT BE KEPT. IT IS INTERESTING TO OBSERVE HOW WRITING IS COMING "FULL CIRCLE," AS SYMBOLS, SUCH AS TEXT MESSAGES, ARE ONCE AGAIN BEING USED AS A MEANS OF COMMUNICATION.

A significant step in writing occurred when graphics began to represent the sounds of spoken language. From the beginning of time, man has recorded his story in pictures, eventually changing the pictures and their sounds to script. The alphabet—not as we know it today, but similar—was invented by the Phoenicians about three thousand years ago during 100–700 BC. Linguists have documented some three thousand different languages in use today throughout the world, but only about a hundred of these are ordinarily written down. Writing has become the universal way for people to record or predict their own history.

Historically it was believed that individuals who could write possessed great power. Centuries ago, very few people could write, and, therefore, the power of the written word was held in the hands of a select few. As citizens of the twenty-first century, we take a lot for granted, including the amazing communication devices that are literally at our fingertips, not fully realizing how the accumulated effect of writing continues to have a significant impact on our culture today as the story of writing continues to evolve.

Some of the first, well-known journalers were Darwin, Lincoln, and Leonardo da Vinci. Darwin and Lincoln were both compulsive scribblers, forever jotting down phrases, notes, and ideas on scraps of paper, stuffing them in a drawer, coat pocket, desk, or even a hat! The story goes that they collected them until they found a use for them. According to Michael Gelb in *How to Think Like Leonardo da Vinci*, the great artist and creative thinker kept a journal with him at all times to jot down ideas, impressions, and observations as they occurred.[2] Gelb estimated that there are about seven thousand pages in his journal notebooks. That is a lot of writing! Many individuals keep similar practice today, taking notes or writing down thoughts, which is a wonderful way to begin the journaling process and capture some of our most spontaneous thoughts. I highly recommend a small notebook for that specific use called a Moleskine. I carry one at all times, jotting down ideas and notes to transfer later into some other format.

The very act of writing is connected with the body. The eyes as well as other senses enter into the dialogue we choose to impart on the page before us. Our desire to write and tell our story or to ask the question *why* is not new. This curiosity has enhanced the evolution of writing. There is another truth that is still rooted in our mass consciousness, and that is that writing contains a certain power, just as it did millions of years ago. The continuous quest to stretch beyond the "known" is the field where writing and journaling lead us. As the poet Rumi wrote,

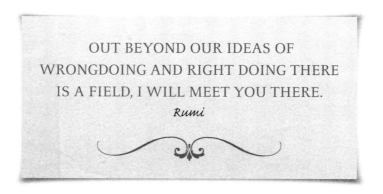

OUT BEYOND OUR IDEAS OF
WRONGDOING AND RIGHT DOING THERE
IS A FIELD, I WILL MEET YOU THERE.

Rumi

Barriers to Journaling

I have identified the three most common barriers to journaling as confidentiality, staring at the blank page, and accessibility. All three of these barriers have to be overcome before an individual can create the safe sanctuary that is paramount to do the important and private work of journaling.

CONFIDENTIALITY:

Much of our writing is emotionally true, but not factually accurate. Sometimes it is explosive, raging, and overreactive. Journaling doesn't usually present the picture of our best selves. If your journaling always presents a pretty picture, something is probably not congruent. There is nothing wrong with writing happy, wonderful things as well as serious things, but if it is always that way, chances are you are not getting to the true picture of yourself and your situation. Confidentiality is key to the journaling process. Sometimes we hold information that would be damaging to ourself or others. To get a clear and honest reflection of ourself and clear the mind, we must be able to express our deepest fears and emotions. When you journal, it should be for an audience of one—yourself.

Recently a friend relayed a story regarding her biggest barrier to journaling: confidentiality. She asked me if others had faced this dilemma. She had gone to her favorite spot in the park and written extensively about a situation she was experiencing at work. It had dredged up old tapes of things that had happened to her many years ago. She was a different person now, but the incident at work seemed to bring up all of the old negative feelings. These were things that she didn't want anyone to know about—ever! Not her children, her friends, or her significant other. She knew that to continue her process, she had to put her journal in a safe place where no one could find it. She chose her closet where it could lie in a box with the other journals underneath several old sweaters she rarely wore. It seemed safe enough. She made a pact with her trusted friend Jane to be the destroyer of the journals if anything happened to either one of them. It may have sounded like a silly pact to others, but, for her, it was the only way she felt safe enough to pour out her heart.

Planning what happens to our private work is important to our feeling of safety in writing. Think about the best options for you. If journaling online appeals to you, some individuals are now storing their journals on password-protected sites or on their own desktops. Thinking about who will be responsible to hit delete if something happens to you is important. Other people choose to get rid of their own journals when they finish a certain period in their lives. I let my journals go after I wrote my memoir. My memoir distilled my journals in a way that later made them superfluous.

This may sound extreme, but confidentiality is really the catalyst to lead us to our own truth. If we have to screen our thoughts, we cannot fully purge our emotional body. To form a new paradigm or picture, we must be able to download all our thoughts, not just the nice ones. Therefore, feeling confident that absolutely no one can read our journal is the first rule of journaling.

QUESTIONS FOR CONTEMPLATION:
- What is the best way for you to journal? Where do you feel safe journaling?

- Do you need to talk to your spouse, significant other, or a parent regarding the confidentiality of journaling?
- Do you have a plan? Think of several different places where you can keep your journals. Make a plan for a safe place for the journals to go should something happen to you. Do not leave this to chance.

STARING AT THE BLANK PAGE:

The second barrier to journaling is staring at the blank page. Many people simply do not know where to begin their story. The reality is you begin your story with wherever you are, with whatever is being presented to you that moment. Some individuals feel like they will do it wrong. Others feel overwhelmed by the enormity of their situation. There is simply no wrong in journaling. When in the midst of a situation, it is helpful to begin with a question, or by describing the situation, and see what answer comes to mind. It doesn't matter how ridiculous the answer sounds. Just write it down. Guided journaling is the process of using a series of questions to help an individual explore a particular situation. Guided journaling is similar to the forward motion in paddling a canoe; as we dip into each question we are pushed forward.

One client, who had a particularly difficult time after her miscarriage, wrote me the following e-mail: "Until I had the questions from your guided journal, I simply did not know where to start. I was too overwhelmed. The questions began to tap into a deeper but more accessible process in me—questions I was afraid to ask myself. They led me into and through my situation. Now I write every day—poems, feelings, and insights. It's as if I am no longer afraid of my feelings. I can manage them and express them through writing. A part of me that had been hiding has opened and has become my new voice."

QUESTIONS FOR CONTEMPLATION:

- Write a word, name a situation, and express a feeling, a burning question, or a thought for the day. Write down any thoughts related to that statement. Take ten to fifteen minutes to do this exercise. Remember that complete sentences, eloquent writing, grammar, and punctuation are all unnecessary. Close whatever you are writing, and don't look at it again until evening. Has it been resolved, or do you have more to write? Have you thought about it again?

- Write more thoughts you have pertaining to this situation.

ACCESSIBILITY:

We cannot always predict when we will need or want to write. My experience has been that thoughts seem to pop in my head at the most inopportune time! Having a way to jot something down is really essential. Little notes help, such as in the Moleskine I mentioned earlier. Although it is an option, it can be cumbersome to carry our journal everywhere with us, and, yet, some people do. Another alternative for many who are on the computer all day is a secure file. Making sure we can access paper or pencil or computer is an important asset of our journaling lives.

Many clients tell me that when they are driving, they have some of their best thoughts—similar to the ones in the shower. One client said that he draws pictures in a Moleskine when stopping at lights, and later transfers these to use as presentation material. Another described her story of being on a trip in the wilds of Africa. She kept a small pad of paper and a pencil in her pocket. She scratched out words and sketches on the paper as a reminder of what she wanted to write about. At the end of her trip, the words triggered her thoughts back to all the amazing adventures that she carried in her mind and heart. This is a great reminder that words, pictures, sounds, taste, and smell all trigger our memory. All of your senses are activated as you write.

QUESTIONS FOR CONTEMPLATION:

- Try several different formats, and see what works for you. Put a small pen and pad of paper in your pocket or purse. Carry it around for several days, and write the words that come to you during the day. Take the words out at the next journaling time, and see how they connect and what meaning they have for you.

- Alternatively, try working on the computer if writing seems too laborious—your mind and body know which is best for you. Write short notes to yourself, and save them during the day. E-mail them to yourself at the end of the day.

Guided vs. Unguided Journaling

It is supremely important, in any type of journaling, not to be an internal editor. Just let the thoughts flow from one page to the next … in fact, when you are not focused on editing, you know you are not in your head, you are in your heart … and that is where journaling takes us.

GUIDED JOURNALING:

Many individuals have difficulty beginning the journaling process. They simply don't know what to write. Guided journaling offers sets of questions that guide the individual through feelings and actions that the individual experiences as a result of the situation. Writing and answering in response to these targeted questions directs the individual toward the inner core of the self to help access information to begin the healing process. Connecting with the inspired consciousness of another person, and exploring questions relative to the experience, may expedite the understanding and reformation of the situation.

UNGUIDED JOURNALING:

Journaling our life experiences as they present themselves to us helps us to not just go through the experience but to find meaning in each of the experiences in our lives. The resulting insight, however, might take place at a later point in time than when the incident was first recorded. Journaling is much more than just recounting facts. It gives us the opportunity to look at specific situations and become the observer of our own behavior, which leads to a conscious awareness of how we are living our lives. One thought triggers another, which is the great healing benefit of journaling. It gives our lives a new dimension as we follow the multicolored threads from one page to the next while we weave the tapestry of our lives.

Blogging vs. Journaling

I am frequently asked to explain the difference between blogging and journaling. Just as writing was the root of our civilization millions of years ago, man continues to have the desire to recount his story today. Currently, in our culture, that takes many shapes and forms. Blogging and journaling have two completely different intentions.

Blogging is sharing the events of your life with multiple or even millions of individuals. It gives the reader information about your likes and dislikes, your ups and downs, and thought processes on a multitude of subjects. That may be therapeutic in some ways to get things off of your mind, but I always try to caution people that everyone has an opinion of what others are doing. Some blogs are amazing stories, but it is done for a different reason than journaling—-it is done to share. Blogging is an external process.

Journaling is an internal process and intended to be private at the time of the writing. That is not to say that there may be parts of your journal that you want to share at some point, but for you to reap the amazing benefits of journaling, it must be something that you intend to keep private or use as a tool for self-discovery. If you are using something as a tool for self-discovery, you do not want the insight of millions of people—it is for you to determine what is right for you. To discover the authentic self, it must come from deep within, not from the opinion of others.

So, it is important to establish your intention before proceeding with the writing that identifies you!

Our Amazing Brain:
The Links to Journaling

Right Brain, Left Brain

*I*N ORDER TO UNDERSTAND WHY JOURNALING WORKS THE WAY IT DOES TO ENABLE US TO MAKE CHANGES, WE MUST UNDERSTAND HOW THE BRAIN WORKS AND THE SEQUENCE OF REACTIONS THAT ARE ACTIVATED IN OUR BODY WHEN WE JOURNAL.

The typical brain has some 100 billion cells, which form a network of more than a quadrillion connections that guide how we communicate, breathe, or move every second. That is a lot of work—that level of power and capacity makes us understand why our potential to achieve what we want is without limit. Wow! But, like anything, we have to know how to harness the power of the brain to use it effectively. So, we will begin with the two hemispheres of the brain, the right hemisphere and the left hemisphere.

The right hemisphere holds the limbic system, which processes the independent streams of information that burst into our brain via the sensory system. The right brain creates the unique picture of what each moment smells like, tastes like, feels like, sounds like, or looks like. These moments of creation are packed with sensations that give us the inventory of the world around us.

The right mind has no sense of time except the present moment. The present moment is our connection to everything being connected as one. Incongruent messages between body language, facial expression, speech, and overall body expression are evaluated by the right brain. The right brain perceives each of us as equal members of the human family. It recognizes similarities, and it is our ability to be empathic. It works well at synthesizing information and perceiving things as a whole.

In contrast, the left hemisphere processes information a different way. It puts together a sequence of time. It organizes the details into a past, present, and future. It thrives on the details, and more details, and more details. It looks at the sequence of order so that we can get a result. It weaves the facts into a story. It is filled with pattern recognition and is superb at predicting what we will think based upon our past experience. Our left hemisphere thinks in patterned responses to incoming stimulation. Brain chatter lies in the left hemisphere. The left brain repeats over and over again the details of your life so you can remember them. It is your ego center. Without the details, you would not know who you are.

The left brain establishes circuits that are connected to the sensory information. Each time a circuit of neurons is stimulated, it takes less stimulation for that circuit to run. The left brain categorizes information into hierarchies, including things that attract and repel us. It analyzes information and places the judgment of good and bad on things we like and dislike. Language resides in the left side of the brain. The left side of the brain is what makes us human.

Understanding these two parts of our brain helps us to understand how we respond to the stimulation coming in through our sensory system during each day. Both halves play a role in nearly everything we do and possess different specialties. Knowing and understanding that, in turn, helps us to understand more about how we operate in the world, and that helps us to use our gifts and talents to our greatest advantage.

The Conscious and the Subconscious

In my training as a therapist, I was taught to understand the basic fundamental functions of the conscious and subconscious parts of the brain. But, as I started to explore why journaling works, I discovered more detailed information which helps us understand the brain's gifts and limitations. With this information, we can learn how to work with both the conscious and the subconscious in order to achieve the desired results to move forward with our vision and dreams. Most individuals want to make changes in their lives; they have the desire, but cannot seem to make the changes happen. Why? The answer lies in the brain, in the conscious and the subconscious.

The conscious mind is the thinking, creative mind that expresses free will. This is the part of the brain that you use when you make new decisions or evaluate various options. The conscious brain has determination, reasoning ability, perception, intuition, and imagination. We identify with our conscious thoughts, but the grand illusion of the conscious is that it cannot follow through. It cannot get things done in the long term. It can plan the menu, but it can't do the cooking. We can come up with great ideas in the conscious, but we cannot sustain them. In our conscious, creative mind, we may consider ourselves as right, or justified, but as we shall see, limiting programs in the subconscious undermine our efforts. We are generally consciously unaware of our fundamental perceptions or beliefs about life.

The subconscious is the power center of the brain. It records everything and remembers everything it experiences forever. It is a stimulus-response device. It is where our beliefs, habits, accomplishments, achievements, and actions reside. According to cognitive neuroscientists, while the conscious brain controls 5 percent or less of our cognitive behavior, most of our decisions, actions, emotions, and behavior are controlled by the subconscious, where 95 percent of our brain activity occurs. The conscious brain processes about 2,000 bits of information per second, and the subconscious brain processes about 400,000,000,000 bits of information per second. It is our basic operating system. Images and behaviors observed by children during the first six years of life are recorded and stored in the subconscious. As we learn to walk, tie our shoes, or drive a car, it becomes rote; we can do it without thinking because the autopilot, the subconscious, is in control. As thoughts and experiences are repeated, certain habits are created in the subconscious, programming our future.

In Bruce Lipton's book *The Biology of Belief*, he states, "If the subconscious mind is programmed with inappropriate behavioral responses to life's experiences, then we will continue to crash in our experiences."[3] In other words, our behavioral program mismanages the body's response to stress. He states that "When the mind perceives that the environment is safe and supportive, the cells are preoccupied with the growth and maintenance of the body." When an individual perceives a situation as stressful, it can cause the mind to malfunction or interfere with its performance, causing a breakdown.

Beliefs are the accumulation of thoughts as they relate to experiences. The misconception is that beliefs represent the truth, and they are not necessarily the truth at all! Beliefs are thoughts that have been recorded through repetition and have become automatic. This is the subconscious control I spoke of earlier: 95 to 98 percent of our habits are automatic. So, how can we begin to change behavior that is driven by those subconscious thoughts and beliefs? In order to change those beliefs we have to change our thought patterns, and that is a function of both the conscious and subconscious.

The conscious mind is the creator, the intuition, the inspiration. We can pick ideas from a large field. But, in order to sustain the idea, it has to be planted in the subconscious brain. Our brain retrieves information, and once information is available or planted in the subconscious, it can be retrieved at any time. That leads to the next step … planting.

Neuroplasticity

Neuroscience has taken a quantum leap in the past few years. Scientists used to believe that the process of cell division that creates new brain cells slowed down in life and stopped altogether by the time we were in our teens. Neuroplasticity is changing all of that. New information tells us that we are making new brain cells and new neural connections all the time. This process of neurogenesis, which is the process of creating new neurons and connections, does not stop in childhood but continues into adulthood. Each time we are having a new thought or experience, we are making a new neural connection. As we have new thoughts, we are carving out new neural pathways in our brain.

The subconscious mind cannot determine whether an experience is real or only imaginary. This gap is the great plus for the conscious. The conscious can create pictures of what we want, and the subconscious cannot determine if it is really happening, or only our imagination. Thoughts are carried along a series of electrical impulses, moving from neuron to neuron, leaping across the gaps or synapses between them. Each time you have the same thought, there is less resistance to that same synaptic leap. You are carving a new pathway. There is an expression in neuroscience that follows, "Neurons that fire together wire together." As you have the same thought pattern over and over, the new neural patterns in your brain literally wire themselves together, providing a place for your new beliefs to be automatically triggered.

In the book *The Answer* by Assaraf and Smith, the authors cite a study at the National Aeronautics and Space Administration (NASA) that tested the physiological and psychological impact of spatial disorientation, the same experience that someone might have during extended time in a weightless environment. "The participants had to wear goggles that turned everything upside down for twenty-four hours a day. The results of this experiment were amazing. After twenty-six days into the experiment the goggles had not changed, but everything turned right side up. What happened? The men's brains had created enough new neural connections to completely rewire their brains, so that their vision and spatial perception worked at 180 degrees from the way the brain normally worked. From this we can conclude that it takes about thirty days of consistently applying neural reconditioning for the unconscious brain to absorb the new information." [4]

So how is journaling impacted by all of this? Because, as we journal, we download our thoughts and feelings, opening the mind to new experiences. As we begin to heal, we can give our attention to the present, which is where new thoughts exist. As we have learned, thoughts wire together to create new neural pathways. As we review the studies on journaling, we will see where all the dots start to connect, and why journaling is such a powerful tool to help us facilitate change and discover who we really are—instead of what someone else programmed us to be.

The Relationship of Cells, Communication, and the Disease Process

In 1997, Candace Pert published a groundbreaking book titled *Molecules of Emotion*. In this book, she explores how the chemicals inside our bodies form an information network, linking mind and body. She stated that "Neuropeptides and their receptors, the biochemicals of emotion, are the messengers carrying information to link the major systems of the body into one unit we call the body-mind connection. The traditional separation of mental processes, including emotions, from the body is no longer valid."[5] Her experiments established that the mind was not focused in the head but was distributed via signal molecules to the whole body. This work helps us understand why we feel sick throughout our body when something triggers us emotionally. It is not just in our head. Repressed emotions are stored throughout the body.

There are countless stories of organ recipients who experience the memories or emotions of the person who donated the organ. Our cells are instilled with memories throughout our bodies. Thoughts create chemicals that physically affect the cells throughout our bodies. Our emotions regulate how we perceive our experiences.

BRAIN WAVES:

There are four types of brain waves which produce different states of being. It is important to understand brain waves, so that we can see where journaling fits, and what it can do for us.

The first is beta, which is where most of us function on a day-to-day basis. Beta is great for absorbing new information or focusing on certain tasks, but we can't stay in beta very long. In beta we are operating at a very fast-paced level—we can burn out very quickly.

The alpha brain waves are associated with relaxation, deep learning, light trances. People who do healing touch or meditation operate in an alpha frequency. This is also where we begin to access the unconscious mind. Access to the quantum field begins with alpha brain waves.

Theta brain waves are associated with dreaming. Increased creativity and the ability to tap into universal intelligence are experienced in this frequency.

Delta brain waves are associated with dreamless sleep. Monks and people with training in meditation access this level and the quantum field.

Understanding what brain wave state we are operating in helps provide another link to the power of journaling. Studies show that we enter into a more relaxed state from journaling. As we enter into the relaxed state, we have the ability to access the alpha brain waves, which help us to touch with the quantum field, the source of all matter and energy.

THE QUANTUM FIELD CONNECTION:

As we explore what journaling can do for us, it is necessary to look at all the possibilities of the mind and what benefits might exist as we journal. As science refines itself, we are realizing that the mind has access to more than we ever before imagined.

In the quantum field, everything that ever was exists. It is the source of all matter and energy. A true, unified field theory of the quantum field is being explored by many notable scientists today. In his book *Ageless Body, Timeless Mind*, Deepak Chopra says, "Because your body emanates electromagnetic frequencies, you are yet another expression of the same field. The pulsations of nerve signals racing along your limbs, the electric charge emitted by heart cells, and the faint field of current surrounding your brain all demonstrate that you are not separate from any form of energy in the universe. Any appearance of separation is only the product of the limitation of your senses, which are not attuned to these energies."[6]

Some scientists even hypothesize that all of our higher cognitive processes result from an interaction with the quantum field. This theory is supported in articles, such as one by Johnjoe McFadden, a professor at the U.K.-based School of Biomedical and Life Sciences at the University of Surrey, who believes that our conscious mind could be an electromagnetic field. McFadden says, "This theory would explain why conscious actions feel so different from unconscious ones—it is because they plug into the vast pool of information already held in the brain's electromagnetic field."[7] Therefore, as the human mind extends its boundaries, like a radio receiver, it is accessing information from the collective consciousness, picking up signals and transmitting them.

I have always believed in a oneness, a connection in the universe of all things, as a manifestation of God's creation. I wrote about that in my first book, *The Only Way Through*. In doing the research for this book, I realized that the scientific experiments being done at this time give creditability and understanding to the belief that there is a life force or collective consciousness flowing through our universe that is accessible at all times, connecting all things. I have also realized that as we identify our thought processes through journaling, it opens another pathway to begin to access that amazing field.

Tying It All Together

Many studies have been done on journaling in the past few years, but some of the most notable have been done by James Pennebaker, PhD, a professor and chairman of the Psychology Department at The University of Texas at Austin. In these studies, he has found that individuals who wrote about traumatic experiences reported more positive moods and fewer illnesses. In addition, improved measures of cellular immune-system function, improved liver enzyme effects among university employees, and fewer visits to the student health center for those writing about painful experiences suggested that confronting traumatic experiences was physically beneficial. Other studies by Pennebaker show that writing influences t-cell growth, lowers heart rates and blood pressure, as well as reduces anxiety.

Another research study at the University of Auckland, by associate professors Keith Petrie and Mark Thomas, showed that "Following writing about their deepest emotions, the level of HIV in the blood reduced in patients with HIV infection. This was associated with an improvement in their immune system," the study notes. "There is clear evidence that writing about emotional issues does help people's immune systems. The improvements aren't as powerful as some drugs we use, and writing cannot be used on its own, but it does appear to improve a patient's health."[8]

In 1992, Pennebaker did a study with the outplacement firm Drake Beam Morin and followed sixty-three professionals who had been laid off from their jobs for an eight–month period while they were assigned to one of three writing conditions.[9] In the experimental condition, participants were instructed to write about their deepest thoughts and feelings about the layoff and about how their lives, personal and professional, had been affected. Participants who wrote about losing their jobs were much more likely to find new ones in the months following the study. In fact, within three months, 27 percent of the experimental participants landed jobs, compared with less than 5 percent of the men who did no writing. By five months after writing, 53 percent of those who wrote about their thoughts and feelings had jobs, compared with only 18 percent of the men in the other conditions. That is pretty amazing!

Postexperimental questionnaires from the disclosure studies indicated that putting upsetting events into words changed how participants dealt with past events and ongoing life circumstances.[10] Various disclosure studies have indicated that encouraging individuals to write or talk about personal upheavals is associated not only with improved physical health but also with reduced absentee rates among employed adults[11] and better classroom performance and long-term elevations in life satisfaction among college students.[12] In addition, expressive writing has been significantly related to long-term stability in romantic relationships.[13]

In other words, when individuals write about deeply personal topics, their immediate biological responses are congruent with those seen among people attempting to relax. Another attribute of expressive writing is that it brings about changes in people's social lives. Writing has been shown to increase working memory, and that these effects last several weeks.[14] After people write about difficult events in their lives, they devote less cognitive effort to them, which allows them to be better listeners, as a friend, or at work.

Sometimes the immediate effect of expressive writing about a trauma can produce distress and a negative mood, but it generally doesn't last more than a few hours, and the long-term effects of writing are enormously beneficial. But, if writing about an event in your life ever feels overwhelming, you should stop. It means it is not the time to do that yet, or that you should seek out a professional who can guide you through the process.

From these studies, we can see that journaling can greatly affect our health, both mental and physical. Looking at the studies of Pennebaker and others, we can understand that writing forces people to stop and reevaluate their life circumstances. All of the cognitive changes that take place when we write create the potential for people to look at their circumstances in a different way. And, it all begins with our thoughts and beliefs and how they are related to the experiences we have in our lives.

PART TWO

The Seven Benefits:
How Journaling Unlocks
The *Wisdom Within*

*O*VER THE YEARS, MANY OF MY CLIENTS HAVE SAID THAT THEY CANNOT JOURNAL BECAUSE THEY "STARE AT THE BLANK PAGE." THESE EXERCISES CONSIST OF QUESTIONS DESIGNED TO HELP YOU BEGIN YOUR PATH TO JOURNALING. THE QUESTIONS ARE INTENDED TO ACT AS THE CATALYST TO HELP YOU TO RELEASE OLD THOUGHT PATTERNS, TO JOURNAL YOUR WAY TOWARD UNCOVERING THE INNER WISDOM THAT RESIDES WITHIN YOU, SO THAT YOU CAN MAKE THE CHANGES THAT TRANSFORM YOUR LIFE. REMEMBER, OUR LIVES CONTAIN MANY LAYERS. THE FIRST TIME YOU DO THESE EXERCISES, YOU MAY JUST BE BEGINNING TO PEEL BACK THESE LAYERS. JOURNALING PROVIDES A CONTAINER FOR YOUR THOUGHTS, A SACRED SPACE WHERE NO ONE BUT THE WRITER IS ALLOWED TO ENTER.

This book and these questions should by no means serve as a replacement for therapy, or seeking counseling, if you need it. If at any time the questions seem to overwhelm you, you should stop. The questions are intended to help you begin to discover a way to make changes and enter into a deeper relationship with your authentic self.

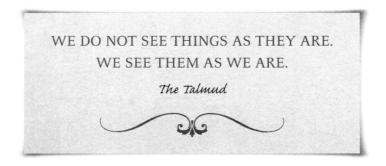

WE DO NOT SEE THINGS AS THEY ARE.
WE SEE THEM AS WE ARE.

The Talmud

Group Work:

Journaling is an internal experience. If these exercises are done in a group, your answers should be confidential unless you choose to share. Sharing could consist of discussing the mental movements and insights that you make in self-reflection, or shifts you notice in your own consciousness to enable you to move forward.

Moving Forward:

As you begin this workbook, set aside a specific time to work on the questions. In my workshops we have a day, and that just helps people begin the process. Scheduling seven weeks to complete the exercises by devoting one section a week to each Benefit gives time for an individual to assimilate the mental shifts that naturally start to occur.

Even though there is room to write underneath the questions, you will probably need more space! Pick out a wonderful journal to use as you begin. Remember, one thought can start a chain of thoughts. This is your story, your work. It's important. If we are ever to give our gifts to the world, it has to come out of our own experiences, not someone else's.

At Work:

There is a separate section for the workplace. This section gives specific examples of how the exercises can be applied in the workplace to understand and enhance your own values, assets, and wisdom, regardless of the work climate surrounding you.

I HAVE OFTEN SAID THAT A PERSON WHO WISHES TO BEGIN A GOOD LIFE SHOULD BE LIKE A MAN WHO DRAWS A CIRCLE. LET HIM GET THE CENTER IN THE RIGHT PLACE AND KEEP IT SO, THEN THE CIRCUMFERENCE WILL BE GOOD.

Meister Eckhart, Sayings

Benefit One:
Health and Wellness

HEALTH IS ONE OF THE BIGGEST BENEFITS WE CAN RECEIVE FROM JOURNALING. RESEARCH HAS SHOWN US THERE IS NO DOUBT THAT THE RELATIONSHIP BETWEEN THE MIND AND THE BODY AND ITS RELATIONSHIP TO THE ENVIRONMENT AND THE UNIVERSE AFFECT EVERYTHING WE DO. MIND, BODY, AND SPIRIT PROGRAMS AND APPROACHES ARE BEING USED IN MOST MAJOR HOSPITALS TODAY. EVEN AFTER ALL OF THIS RESEARCH, WE STILL QUESTION, "DOES THE SIMPLE ACT OF WRITING REALLY MAKE A DIFFERENCE?"

After the death of my husband many years ago, I started to write. I did not write because anyone told me to or because I thought it was a trend. I wrote out of sheer desperation. Something in my intuition told me that if I wrote, I wouldn't go crazy. Something told me that it would give me a sense of control when everything seemed totally out of control. My friends could only listen to so much. I had to find a way to vent. At that time, no one even talked about writing as a modality of healing. I had always been drawn to writing. I had a diary when I was younger. I had stopped writing in high school because of a teacher who informed me I would never be able to really write—and I believed her! With the catastrophic onset of my husband Tom's illness and his death, I knew I had to somehow keep track of all the events swirling around in my head. My intuition was right.

I started keeping a little notebook inside of my purse. I wrote at every doctor appointment and in the waiting rooms. I started writing at night, after Tom and the children were in bed. I wrote pages on yellow legal pads and in journals. I could vent and cry and wake up the next morning and feel more clear and grounded. On the days I wrote, I knew that I had made it through yet another day, and that the events of the day had not made me crazy, not yet! My emotions did not seem to control me. On the days I wrote, I could show up and be present at the next situation and not glaze over. When I became a therapist and started to delve into the world of exploring the mind, I began to realize that the body is merely a recipient of our continual programming from the mind. The mind is programmed by our experiences and our interpretation and reaction to those experiences, which create certain chemicals in our bodies. Why did I feel better after writing? Research has given us those answers.

When we don't do something to take care of ourselves, the outcome can be quite different from when we do. My client Mary had this experience to which many people might relate. When she walked into my office, she didn't resemble the Mary I had seen the year before. She had called after she was released from the hospital for bleeding stomach ulcers. This vibrant, beautiful woman looked pale, and her eyes could hardly meet my gaze, filling with tears as she started to talk. This last year her life had gotten out of control. It started when her husband had lost his company. She had tried to be supportive of him but needed to attend to the other parts of her life already in motion. Her son was getting married, and she was in the middle of planning; she had even reserved the place for the rehearsal dinner. Yet how was she going to do this with the enormous drop in her husband's salary? Her oldest daughter was in college, and Mary was determining how they were going to keep her there. As she attended to everyone's needs, she dismissed and buried her own feelings.

She felt as if she would be betraying her family, or wouldn't seem strong, if she wasn't supportive. She saw several things that could be done about her husband's business, but he was so distraught that she was afraid to even broach the subject with him. She buried everything deeper and deeper until one morning, she could not get out of bed and collapsed on the floor. She almost died in the hospital, but with great care and attention, she had gotten better. She knew clearly that her body would not make it through another experience like this one. She had to figure out a way to download the thoughts that were bombarding her.

We all have situations that life deals us over which we have no control, and yet we need to get a sense of control to regain our footing. I gave Mary some exercises to do that started her on the path to journaling. Downloading the thoughts that ran though her subconscious daily was the first step toward changing the flow of her thoughts. Changing the flow of her thoughts and beliefs was the first step toward changing the outpouring of stressful chemicals, such as cortisol, into her body. Sometimes taking care of ourselves may mean setting aside some of the demands and expectations of others.

Most situations overwhelm us because the circumstances seem bigger than we are. We have a sense that there are no answers. But, when we break down the situation, it gives us choices and a sense of control. The choices may not be the exact ones that we want, but they are a door to the next place. Sometimes we recognize a choice we have had before that didn't turn out very well. When a choice is presented to us again, it is usually an opportunity for us to handle it differently.

The exercises below are designed to move you through stressful situations in your life that are bombarding your body with negative chemicals. By journaling, you begin to download the situation, so that you can look at it differently and gain a new perspective. It is also important for us to recognize when our bodies are in stress and what that stress is doing to us physically. Sometimes we stay in stress so long, it feels like our "new normal." These exercises are intended to heighten your awareness of the different sensations you feel in your body when you move it out of stress and into a positive place. Let's get started on the path to becoming healthy!

Exercises:

HEALTH BENEFITS

1. *Close your eyes and ... Breathe, ... again, ... again, ... again!*

2. Become aware of your body. We all have many situations that give us stress. Think about one stressful situation that you are dealing with now. How does your body feel? Where are you carrying your stress? This is your body's reaction to this stress. Journal/write how your body *feels* when you think about the situation or a particular aspect of that situation that gives you stress.

3. Write about the stressful situation. Describe it as if you were talking to someone.

4. What are the blocks in your path that are preventing you from solving this stressful situation? Journal/write about the blocks.

5. You are standing in your future looking back on the year. As you look back, what do you see clearly that you wish you had done differently about this stressful situation? Describe that.

6. Now, think about the blocks you wrote about in question 4 that are keeping you from moving through this stressful situation. Now that you have a picture of what you wish you had done differently, how could you work *with* the blocks differently than you are now? All movement begins with small steps. What small steps can you make now? Write about these small steps.

7. Ideally, how would you like to see the situation resolved? Journal/write about that.

To move forward to make things happen differently, I am going to move you mentally to a different place ... Are you ready? Let your new thoughts start bubbling ...

When was the last time your body felt free, alive, energized? When you were a child? Adult? Bring up this memory and write about it now. As you write about this memory, think about the positive, good chemicals cascading to all the cells throughout your body.

8. Think about this memory every day. You want to reactivate the chemicals connected to this memory and all of the good feelings and mental pictures that go with this memory. Wow! Journal about this memory again.

9. What could give you this same feeling in the present? Write about a situation that could be possible, which you would like to see happen, that would give you those same good feelings. Write about this as often as you can, every day if possible. It is important to be clear and specific, and keep expanding the idea as you journal. As you journal, construct mental pictures to reflect this situation.

10. Cut out some pictures that represent this happy, past feeling and your new, desired situation that would help you reexperience this feeling in the present. Put them on a board, or make a screensaver of these pictures where you can see them every day. As you repeat the images, you are filling your body and cells with new, powerful, positive chemicals and brain reinforcement.

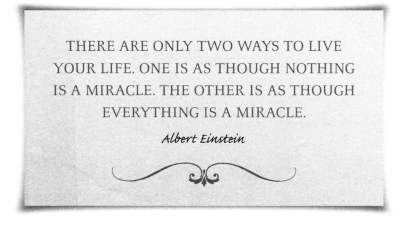

THERE ARE ONLY TWO WAYS TO LIVE
YOUR LIFE. ONE IS AS THOUGH NOTHING
IS A MIRACLE. THE OTHER IS AS THOUGH
EVERYTHING IS A MIRACLE.

Albert Einstein

11. Journal/write about how you would be different if what you want manifested itself, and you felt this way every day.

12. Write to your Muse.

The word *muse* is taken from Greek mythology. Ancient Roman or Greek writers would often begin their poems by asking for the aid of the Muses in their competitions. The word *muse* means "to inspire." The Muse helps us tell our own story. So, take the time to journal to your Muse for at least fifteen to thirty minutes every day. Ask your Muse the most important question that is stirring in your mind. Your Muse may take the form of God, Spirit, Higher Self, Jesus, Buddha, or some other guide. Expect to get an answer.

Benefit Two:
Awareness

*T*HE SECOND BENEFIT THAT PEOPLE RECEIVE FROM JOURNALING IS AWARENESS, THE "AHA." IT'S LIKE FINALLY WAKING UP AND ENTERING A PLACE OF HIGHER CONSCIOUSNESS ABOUT YOUR LIFE. AWARENESS IS RECOGNITION OF A SITUATION, WHICH GIVES US INSIGHT INTO HOW WE ARE PROCESSING THE SITUATION. IF A SITUATION IS NOT IN OUR AWARENESS, WE ARE UNCONSCIOUS ABOUT HOW WE ARE HANDLING IT. PEOPLE WHO ARE NOT AWARE ARE USUALLY PREOCCUPIED OR OPERATING BY "ROTE." WE GET UP, GO TO WORK, COME HOME, EAT DINNER, GO TO BED, GET UP, AND DO IT ALL OVER AGAIN. THERE IS NO TIME OR ENERGY FOR A NEW THOUGHT. SOME ROTE BEHAVIOR IS NECESSARY, LIKE DRIVING A CAR. IF YOU ARE OPERATING ON ROTE, IT MEANS THAT YOU ARE OPERATING FROM THE SUBCONSCIOUS— OPERATING BASED ON OLD THOUGHTS AND BELIEFS.

The first step to changing a stuck, worn-out pattern is awareness of the pattern. Awareness of a situation helps us to focus attention on the situation. Most people want to have good lives. No one has ever walked into my office and said, "I don't want to have a good life." That has never happened!

Therefore I know that most people want to gain the awareness about how to make the most of their lives. Most everyone has periods in life when they are simply unaware. We all do. Remember, we have sixty thousand thoughts a day, and most of these are repetitious! So the question is, how can we become more aware and generate new thoughts ... the old ones are keeping us in the same position we have been in for years. If you have picked up this book, there must be something that you want to change.

One of the first steps in becoming aware is to identify when we are operating in the present, and when we are simply operating from old tapes. True change begins with the ability to align with the present moment. It is the ability to be in alignment with what is happening, not resisting what is happening. The ego resists change, because change knocks it off its pedestal, taking away its control. When we stay attached to an old identity, such as a person we divorced, or a title from an old job, the ego is trying to keep us there. The ego loves control and wants us to believe that if we let go, we will never get there again. So, awareness begins with trying to stay in the present, and sometimes that is not easy.

Becoming aware of and identifying our losses is another component of becoming the authentic self we want to be. Loss is a central theme that transgresses everyone's life at different times. The loss can be from a divorce, death, illness, job change, move, change in a relationship, or retirement. We are not the same person before the loss as we become after a loss. A loss opens the door to the next unknown place in our lives—a place that provides the opportunity to heal wounds and create a new definition of ourselves. But, we must take the time look at our losses and understand their meaning in our lives. One loss can trigger another loss, and many people minimize or do not understand the enormity of their losses and how they impact their day-to-day functioning. Loss can make us feel vulnerable, so we need to be gentle with ourselves. Awareness of our losses is essential to moving forward in our lives.

Our wounds are another area we need to explore as we are becoming aware. A wound is something that has happened to us that has not healed. When someone says or does something that touches our wound, we usually get defensive, angry, or have some other strong reaction. If we are afraid of being vulnerable to someone, there is probably a fear that our wound will be opened, so we keep our distance to keep from getting hurt. Awareness of our wounds helps us to open ourselves to the process of healing.

Awareness calls us to a new way of being in the world. Think about how small children are always interacting with their environment. Their whole bodies are acutely aware of everything around them. They laugh spontaneously, curiosity beckons them, and any part of the sensory system that is activated responds. They have not yet learned to shut down. So, let us begin the process to open ourselves back up, and allow our sensory system to engage again with the world around us.

Let me share with you Jane's story, which is a great example of coming into awareness. Jane is a woman in her late forties who came in to see me. She started telling me the story of how she had been living in the shadow of her divorce for the past ten years. She was angry and bitter that the life she had envisioned, with the money, prestige, and all that went with it, had been taken away. In addition, she had felt like a victim because of the settlement in the divorce, and she felt that she had never recovered financially. She had spent much of her time focusing on her feelings of victimization by her husband. She had created a "story" that said that if you were divorced, you were poor at relationships, and she blamed him for the failure of their marriage. She also believed that it would be very difficult to ever have what she wanted without her ex-husband's income. So, in essence, it was his fault her life had not worked out. Even though she did not call herself a victim, the story she created was telling her just that. She could not understand why she was so unhappy and not able to have the life she wanted.

As she started to journal and reflect on her "stuckness," she realized that she was repeating a family belief that had played out in her family for years. Her mother had felt victimized in her own divorce and had passed this belief on to Jane. Her mother had carried with her the story of her own life never working, and never having enough money because of Jane's father. She completely blamed him for not having the life she wanted, and now Jane was living out her mother's story through her own feelings of victimization.

With journaling as her tool, the patterns that had held her captive emerged onto the pages. She had been resisting the change to no longer be a victim, which continued to tie her to her ex-husband and her old identity. As she explored her thoughts, she began to identify other beliefs that were also false but impacted her actions, choices, and decisions on a daily basis. She realized that she was operating off of old tapes and an old ego identity. Letting go of the past meant that she would have to start to take responsibility for herself in the present, which no longer tied her to her mother's belief, or the identity of her ex-husband. As she aligned with the present, everything started to change.

When intention, passion, alignment, and creativity meet, the universal force is drawn into our field, and an explosion happens ... and it all starts with journaling. So, let's explore what can bring you into the present.

Exercises:
AWARENESS
1. *Close your eyes and ... Breathe, ... again, ... again, ... again!*
2. Write down a situation that you are struggling with, or that you want to change that makes you unhappy or discontent. This might be a relationship, your job and/or career, finances, family situation, living situation, or other.
3. How long have you struggled with this situation? Explain.
4. What is your "story" about this situation, and why it is the way it is, or can't change? Journal/write about that.
5. What are the *unconscious* thoughts or "rote" tapes that feed my discontentment that continue in my head and feed my "story" when I think about this situation? Journal/write these down.
6. What patterns do you see in this situation that remind you of a pattern

in your family? Write down these patterns. Remember, thoughts trigger other thoughts. You may think of more to journal about.

7. Every time I think about this situation I feel _____ (angry, misunderstood, anxious, depressed, unhappy, victimized, stuck, or other).

8. Is there a way to look at this situation differently? Remember, we can't change another person, but we can change the way we look at things. What is a new, *conscious* way you could look at this situation? A *conscious* thought aligns you with the present. In other words, use new words to describe the old story.

    For example, Jane's story: "I am no longer just an ex-wife of Henry who got the shaft. I am Jane, and my freedom gives me the opportunity to explore my own gifts that I want to give to the world." Same story, new words.

Write a new, *conscious* thought that could describe the situation differently, and change the story.

Journal/write the new story as you would like it to be.

LOSS:

Most of us have experienced a loss or multiple losses in our lives. As you explore the losses in your life, remember a loss can be a career, job, divorce, relationship, death, move, or illness. One loss can trigger other losses.

9. Identify your losses. Write a list of the losses in your life.

10. Identify the biggest or most important loss you have experienced. What feelings does the change or loss bring up for you? (Fear, vulnerability, anger, etc.) Journal/write about these feelings now.

11. Is there a loss you are still preoccupied with? What is the preoccupation in your head?

12. Name some of the losses or changes you have navigated in the past. We all have strengths to get through things. Write about how you handled

these losses and what strengths you used to get through these losses.

13. The past can only be healed in the present. Journal/write about how it feels to be here now, even if it's difficult.

14. Journal/write about how you can take care of yourself while dealing with this loss.

15. The loss is *part* of your identity, but not *all* of your identity. Journal/write about how you can move forward in your life, incorporating the loss.

DECISIONS:

Contemplate decisions which have been made in your life. There have been major decisions in your life that defined you. These are turning points in your path that led you in a specific direction. Some of these decisions may have seemed right, others may have led to important lessons, and other decisions you may regret.

16. What decisions were made *for you* that have helped define you?

17. What decisions did *you make* that have helped define you?

18. Which decisions have impacted your identity, "who you are," the most?

IDENTITY:

Who am I? Not a simple question. If our cells are regenerating themselves every day, I am not the same person today as I was three years ago, or even last year! Science has shown that we continue development throughout our adult lives as our brains continue to change. As you have more and more experiences, you change with each experience. Decisions impact our identity. Identity builds. It is important to reflect on certain parts of ourselves that we value and treasure, as well as identify new parts of ourselves that are growing. Keep this in mind as you reflect on the question of identity.

19. Identity: How would you describe your identity five years ago, ten years ago? Journal/write about that person.

20. What situations have made you change or redefine your identity? What does your new identity look like now? What are the important parts

of your old identity that you have kept? Journal/write about that new identity now.

What drives our behavior?

As we explore our motivation for doing something, that process can shift our awareness to become more conscious of our actions, and we can use our actions to benefit ourselves and others. We can be driven by both positive and negative emotions, which affect the outcome of what we do. Also, the degree to which something "drives" us is important.

For example: If I am driven by fear, a little fear could motivate me to do better; or, if taken too far, fear could cause me to steal, lie, or compromise my integrity in other negative ways.

21. What drives your behavior? Fear, loss, depression, perfection, love, helping others, money, other? Identifying what drives our behavior helps us understand and become more conscious of our actions, and if they are coming from a positive place or a negative place.
    a) Write about what drives your life, your behavior.
    b) Write about what happens when you allow yourself to be driven too far. Journal/write about what you can do to manage your behavior before it goes further than you want it to.

What touches our wounds or triggers our behavior?

We all have wounds. Wounds are sensitive places that lie within each of us. If a wound is not yet healed, someone else's actions or words can trigger our wound, causing a strong reaction in us; when someone says or does something that touches that sensitive place, we react. Certain situations can cause strong emotions and reactions in us. In order to heal a wound, it is important to look at the feelings it brings up in us. Self-awareness of when we feel vulnerable or have strong emotional reactions to a situation helps us to be mindful of our wounds that need healing.

On a good day, we can keep our emotions in check, and on a not-so-good day, we cannot. As we explore who we really are, we need to understand what touches or opens our wounds. Becoming aware of what triggers our behavior, or provokes a strong emotion in us, helps us to monitor how we choose to react, and move forward to heal.

22. What triggers or elicits a strong emotion in you? Old wounds, losses, beliefs, fear, control, other? Identifying when you have a strong reaction to someone else will give you an awareness and insight into the wounds in you that need to heal. If people are walking on eggshells around you, it is possible you are getting triggered very easily. Awareness of our own responses to things and situations that provoke us or elicit a strong reaction is key to changing our own behavior or acknowledging the wounds that need to heal.

    Journal/write about what triggers your behavior or causes a strong emotional reaction in you, and what you can do to manage yourself. Can you identify the wound that this touches in you? Write about that.

23. What are the Ahas you have discovered? Write a list of these.

24. Write to your Muse
    Journal/write to your Muse for fifteen to thirty minutes every day. Ask your Muse to help you create a new story. It may not happen all at once ... stories unfold. Keep journaling and ask your Muse to guide you. Keep a Moleskine notebook in your pocket—you never know when the Muse will appear!

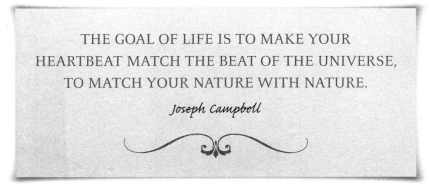

THE GOAL OF LIFE IS TO MAKE YOUR
HEARTBEAT MATCH THE BEAT OF THE UNIVERSE,
TO MATCH YOUR NATURE WITH NATURE.

Joseph Campbell

Benefit Three:
Connection—
Understanding and Experiencing
Our Connection to All Things

*I*N MY FIRST BOOK, *THE ONLY WAY THROUGH*, I WROTE ABOUT MY CONNECTION TO ALL THINGS, AND HOW MY REALIZATION OF "ONENESS" BUILT OVER TIME. IT DIDN'T HAPPEN ALL AT ONCE. IT SEEMED THAT THE MORE AWARE I BECAME OF THAT CONNECTION TO ONENESS, EXPERIENCES PRESENTED THEMSELVES TO HELP ME UNDERSTAND THAT. MANY OPPORTUNITIES HAD PROBABLY BEEN PRESENTED TO ME BEFORE TO EXPERIENCE ONENESS, BUT I COULDN'T ACKNOWLEDGE THEM, BECAUSE I WASN'T AWARE OF THE ARRAY OF CONNECTION IN EVERYTHING THAT EXISTS. THAT WAS ONE OF MY AHAS!

My experience with oneness began with my husband Tom's last breath, as if I was breathing with him as I watched him take that last breath. It continued when I stepped into a remote creek, and my eyes locked with a beautiful deer standing so close I could feel his breath, and, in similar moments, when I felt enveloped by this same feeling, such as when I connected with the people at the grief center where I worked. These experiences have continued as I have engaged in certain types of prayer, meditation, yoga, listened to certain music, and the list goes on and on. As I have become aware of oneness, I realize it happens all the time. Being fully present to others is a way to experience oneness.

This last year, I took an amazing trip to Morocco. This developing country is connecting the past and the future. There are donkeys carrying Coca-Cola, or loads of goods on their backs, traveling beside Mercedes vans carrying passengers to various parts of the region. As we climbed the narrow, rocky paths to the ancient villages in the Atlas Mountains, we observed the Berber mountain children running the dusty mountain trails in sandals.

As they run past, we catch glimpses of them. Their gaze meets ours, and their bright, shining eyes lock in curious, friendly glances as they stare through us, the strangers in their world. Our languages are different but the eyes tell the story—the eyes, the windows of the soul. They are completely present to everything around them—nature, animals, the earth, and people. They miss nothing and are not afraid of connecting.

This is the same connection I felt years earlier with the deer, and which I have felt with people who know how to be present—a connection, a oneness.

In the world of quantum physics, matter and energy are proven to be completely connected. As we understand more about how we fit into the environment, we can grasp that we are all made of cells, atoms, and molecules that have frequencies that connect to everything else in this magnificent universe. Through the amazing work being done by many scientists, as well as by spiritual people, we are fortunate to be the recipients of new information to help us understand how to make more positive changes than have ever before been possible.

As we begin to explore oneness and connection, we have to give attention to the sensory system, which processes all the information that comes to us from our environment. As the senses are activated, it launches a chain of events that triggers our thoughts, emotions, and beliefs, which, in turn, determine our values and how we respond and interact in the world. Ultimately, we explore our divine connection with God, spirituality, and nature, which determines our connection with everything that exists.

Exercises:
CONNECTION—UNDERSTANDING AND EXPERIENCING OUR CONNECTION TO ALL THINGS

Sensory:
EXPLORING THE SENSES

The right hemisphere of the brain holds the limbic system, which processes the independent streams of information that burst into our brain via the sensory system. We can all become caught in the emotional loops that run in our brain. Whether it is grief, loss, anger, joy, or any other emotion, the circuit will be triggered by the sensory system from the right brain.

Many of the clients whom I have seen in my practice have had a lot of loss. One of the stories I frequently hear is how difficult it is to go to the grocery store after a loved one has passed away. It was one of the most difficult things for me after the loss of my husband. I walked into the grocery store, started crying, and had to leave. Going to the grocery store is like a ritual for many families. I realized all of the things I no longer needed to buy. The sensory system gets highly activated by the sense of smell and the visuals surrounding you. Going to the grocery store activates our whole body.

Certain sounds, pictures, smells, and other information coming into us from the environment activate the sensory system. Become more aware of your sensory activation as you journal through the following questions.

1. *Close your eyes and ... Breathe, ... again, ... again, ... again!*

2. Describe a situation when you were "triggered" by your senses. What "old tape" did it bring up in your awareness? Describe.

3. Name the four people or animals in your life that you feel connected to. What connects you to each person or animal? Describe.

4. Name two to four places you feel connected to. What connects you to each place? Journal and describe those places.

5. Our sensory system is what makes us feel connected to everything else. Describe a time when you have felt connected to everything that existed.

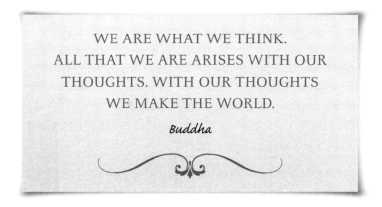

WE ARE WHAT WE THINK.
ALL THAT WE ARE ARISES WITH OUR
THOUGHTS. WITH OUR THOUGHTS
WE MAKE THE WORLD.

Buddha

Thoughts:

Thoughts are created as we move through the environment around us and our sensory system is activated. Thoughts are the most influential force we have in our lives. Thoughts repeated over and over become beliefs, and beliefs become habits. So, becoming aware of our thoughts is the first step in the process of becoming present. Our thoughts determine who we are and what we do in the world. Our actions follow our thoughts. Our thoughts are attached to emotions. Our inner thoughts can become our intentions, which is why we must monitor our thoughts.

A client recently told me a story about buying yogurt. She was standing at the checkout counter at the grocery store and realized with frustration that she had bought plain yogurt instead of the vanilla she had intended to buy. She started asking herself how she could make such a stupid mistake; how could she be so dumb! She was genuinely upset. This overreaction connected her thought immediately back to a childhood experience when her mother had chastised her for buying the wrong milk and paying ten cents too much for the milk. The yogurt incident activated her sensory system and the story she had stored about the milk.

Our thoughts build our stories from their attachment to certain neural pathways in our brain. As we learn to be aware of the thoughts in our head, we can learn to stop some of the negative tapes that seem to just "run." We have to be conscious of our thoughts in order to change them.

6. Listen to chatter in your head. For one day, try to monitor this chatter. When a negative thought or self-talk comes, think about what part of your sensory system is activated and what belief is attached to the thoughts. Write about what happens when you have a negative thought.

7. Write what the "truth" is about that thought pattern and the belief system that needs to change.

Emotions:

In Jill Bolte Taylor's book *My Stroke of Insight*, she describes how we respond to stimulation coming in through our sensory system during each day. Dr. Taylor says, "There are certain limbic system programs that can be triggered automatically, and it takes less than 90 seconds for one of these programs to be triggered, surge through our body, and then be completely flushed out of the blood stream."[15] She cites anger as one of the programmed responses that can be set off automatically. She says that once triggered, within ninety seconds from the initial trigger, the chemical component of anger has completely dissipated from the blood, and the automatic response is over. It is then, she says, that we have a choice either to hook back into the neurocircuitry or move back into the present moment, allowing the reaction to melt away.

8. Think about the experience that Taylor has described in the paragraph above. We all have emotions that get triggered automatically. It is important to acknowledge them and learn to manage them. Think of a situation that made you angry, close your eyes, and time yourself. See if you can let this situation run through your system for ninety seconds and move on to something else, a new thought—a present thought. If you cannot "let go" after ninety seconds, use this as information to explore this situation a little further by journaling/writing about it. Keep this exercise in your awareness and try it tomorrow when someone triggers something else in you. It is a great way to practice managing your emotions. It's a choice!

9. Cut a few pictures out of a magazine that attract you. Pick one picture out of the group of pictures. Look at the picture that you picked. Think about how this picture speaks to you.

Write about what meaning this picture holds for you, what thoughts it brings into your mind, and the emotions it brings up in you.

BELIEF SYSTEMS:

What you believe in your mind absolutely affects your biology and your actions. Once the subconscious mind accepts perceptions of something as "truth," it is hardwired into our own brains, becoming our "truth." Our thoughts create our truths. Consequently, programmed misconceptions in our subconscious mind are not "monitored" and can engage us in limited thinking and old, restrictive behaviors.

One of my belief systems when my husband died was that if you were not a stay-at-home mom, your children would simply not turn out right. My mother, sweet and well intentioned, had passed that belief on to me. When I went back to work after Tom's death and experienced a positive outcome from working, it rendered the old belief system that I had lived with seem completely incorrect. I then changed my thoughts to construct and support a new belief system that supported what I was doing and worked in my life.

When we have an experience, our response to the experience records a positive or negative outcome in our subconscious brain. The universe has a wonderful way of presenting situations to us again so that we can experience something in a new way. That sometimes requires us to change our belief systems. When we "let go" and allow ourselves to reexperience something in a new way, it helps us to change a belief system and move forward differently. It "heals" old wounds or beliefs and enables us to behave differently.

Here are a few examples of belief systems that I have encountered from clients who were stuck:

- My job is just to make money.
- If I do not get a certain grade or get into a specific school, I will be a failure.
- If I leave this job, I will never find another one.
- I could never make more than $_____ a year.
- I always fail at relationships.
- I am a terrible parent because _____.
- I am irresponsible because I am sometimes late.

10. Name a belief system (or more than one) that you have lived out of that might be judgmental to yourself or make you judge others. Journal/write about that.

11. What would happen if you changed that belief system?

12. What is a belief you have that might be released or changed to help you with an issue you cannot resolve? Journal/write about the issue and the belief system.

13. What is a belief that you might need to release or change for your path/ story to unfold in a different way? Journal/write about that belief and how your story/life could change if you release that belief.

14. What is a belief system that has kept you from connecting with certain

people or groups? How would your life or relationships change if that shifted or changed? (Example: I am not good enough to _____).

> YOU HAVE A SILENT PARTNERSHIP WITH THE INFINITE. REST IN THIS DIVINE ASSURANCE AND THIS DIVINE SECURITY. THIS IS MORE THAN A SENTIMENT. KNOW THAT THE SPIRIT FLOWS IN TRANSCENDENT LOVELINESS INTO YOUR WORLD OF THOUGHT AND FORM, THAT IT FLOWS THROUGH YOUR WHOLE BEING, SPIRITUAL, EMOTIONAL, MENTAL AND PHYSICAL.
>
> *Ernest Holmes*

Meditation and Spirituality:

As we explore connections, meditation and spirituality are the highest connection to everything that is possible. Without understanding and exploring our own personal connection to God, the Universe, or a Higher Power, we operate as a closed system. Journaling is a way to open our minds and become the observer of our lives in the context of the greater world and to explore at a deeper level what is our own understanding and relationship with God, the Universe, or Higher Power.

When I meditate, I go into a space of oneness with God. My breathing takes over, and I simply try to let my mind go blank. It is my time to listen. I usually try to write before or after I meditate. It is important for me to capture some thoughts before I go blank. It is sometimes helpful to write before you meditate, as it helps to download the "monkey mind" that seems to plague us when we become silent. Meditation helps me expand my consciousness and deepen my relationship with God.

Nature also helps me expand my understanding and relationship with God. No matter how separate things appear, nothing is separate when we immerse our minds into the field of everything that exists and connects around us.

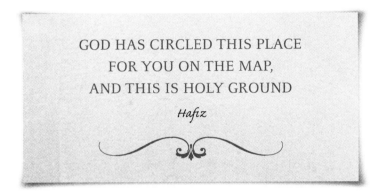

GOD HAS CIRCLED THIS PLACE
FOR YOU ON THE MAP,
AND THIS IS HOLY GROUND

Hafiz

Exercises:

15. When do you feel closest to God? Describe the time when you have that feeling.

16. Is there one incident that has drawn you closer to God, or pushed you away? Journal/write about what happened.

17. Are you in the process of defining or redefining your own spirituality? What has happened to make you want to do that? Write about what would help you to do that.

18. What do you need to change in your life to allow yourself to become closer to God/Spirit/Higher Power? Journal/write about what conscious actions you think you might be able to make to do that.

19. Pick a time when you can sit in nature, be silent, and write. Write about your connection to nature, describe the spot where you chose to write, and

your connection to all things.

20. Write to your Muse: journal/write to your Muse for fifteen to thirty minutes or more each day. Spirituality is not meant to be separate from the body or mind. Ask your Muse how to integrate your awareness and experience of Spirit into every moment of your everyday life.

Benefit Four:
Focus

WHEN WAS THE LAST TIME YOU REALLY FOCUSED ON ONE THING? OUR CULTURE IS ADOPTING MULTITASKING AS THE NEW NORMAL. WHEN YOU ARE MULTITASKING, YOU ARE MISSING INFORMATION. WE HAVE BILLIONS OF BITS OF INFORMATION THAT COME INTO OUR BRAIN VIA OUR SENSORY SYSTEM; WHEN YOU MULTITASK, YOU ARE MISSING 99 PERCENT OF IT. THUS, IN MEETINGS WHERE EVERYONE IS CHECKING E-MAIL AND TEXT MESSAGING, OPPORTUNITIES FOR CONCENTRATION, CREATIVE EXPLORATION, AND CRITICAL THINKING ARE LOST. WHETHER AT HOME OR AT WORK, INATTENTION GIVES A CLEAR MESSAGE: "YOU ARE NOT WORTH MY TIME."

Certain situations such as loss, illness, or death have the capacity to make us preoccupied and lose focus. Have you ever felt like thoughts are running through your mind? The typical response I hear is that "I cannot seem to get out of the conversation in my head. I almost ran a red light. My head is completely preoccupied with my situation." This response is especially prevalent when someone tries to push away thoughts about loss, or some situation they are grappling with, and not deal with it. Our mind fills us with chatter, a conversation that is with one person, yourself.

Journaling is a way for us to download the chatter in the mind—to empty the "in box." Journaling our thoughts out on paper or on a computer is a way to contain the thoughts and stop the chatter. As we download our thoughts on paper or into a file on the computer, we can let them go, knowing they will be held there for us to process at another time. The job of the mind is to help us remember. Journaling helps the mind to know we are holding the thought, similar to hitting the save button on the computer, with the reassurance that the thoughts will not be lost, and we can return when we choose to do so.

One of the greatest benefits from journaling is the ability to focus and continue to maintain that focus. Studies done by Pennebaker show us that the grades of students who journal actually improve after journaling. Journaling helps us to calm the "monkey mind" and these thoughts that race through our heads. In addition, the writing is slowing the surge of negative chemicals throughout our bodies, which makes us feel better physically.

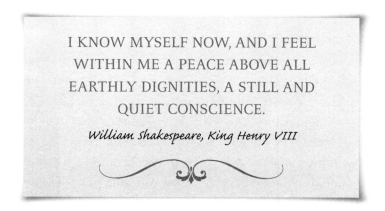

I KNOW MYSELF NOW, AND I FEEL
WITHIN ME A PEACE ABOVE ALL
EARTHLY DIGNITIES, A STILL AND
QUIET CONSCIENCE.

William Shakespeare, King Henry VIII

Many studies have been done on "balance" in people's lives. What we focus on and give our attention to is what grows stronger in our lives. It is difficult to maintain balance and focus when we are not intentional about operating in the conscious and are unaware of our own patterns and actions. Without focus, it is easy to fall back into old habits.

As individual thinking is streamlined, the avalanche of tasks can be brought into focus and managed. Each task can flow into harmony with the present moment as we reach into the caverns of our minds, connecting our thoughts with the surrounding environment, one task at a time.

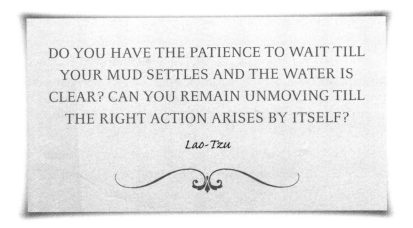

> DO YOU HAVE THE PATIENCE TO WAIT TILL
> YOUR MUD SETTLES AND THE WATER IS
> CLEAR? CAN YOU REMAIN UNMOVING TILL
> THE RIGHT ACTION ARISES BY ITSELF?
>
> *Lao-Tzu*

Exercises: Focus

MONKEY MIND:

My client Katie was a typical example of someone who had difficulty shutting down the thoughts that would not stop after a sudden loss. She had tried to return to work after being off for three days. She relayed her story of trying to return to work after the death of her daughter. She said that she almost had a wreck on the way to work. Her mind was still consumed with the details of every part of her daughter's recent death. It was as though her mind was grappling with trying to remember the details of the horrific last few weeks. She stated that throughout the day, she would find herself sitting at her desk and just staring at the computer screen. It was as if she was in a trance. She was thinking about all of the things that had happened when Mary was a little girl. She was retracing every part of her life. She was also very anxious and finding that everything that anyone said or did irritated her. Why was she even back here? Her whole body felt sick most of the time. Her boss was a very patient person, but he clearly did not understand the enormity of what she had been through. What could she do? She knew that she couldn't take off from work indefinitely. The conversation in her head would not end.

Whether we are stressed about work, or a relationship, or a sudden loss, we all feel that we should be able to return to normal after a crisis in our lives. The truth is, our sensory system is on overload. We cannot begin to process everything that has happened to us. Our body and mind are saying, "I need time. I am in shock." We need time to integrate all the pieces that are new information. What we knew as "truth" is no longer a part of our lives.

As you begin the exercises below, let your thoughts flow out onto the pages. It might take several days, or even weeks to regain focus. But, it will happen.

1. *Close your eyes and ... Breathe, ... again, ... again, ... again!*

2. What are the thoughts that are "running" through your mind at this moment? It might be several different situations, topics, subjects, or feelings. Whatever those thoughts are, take at least fifteen minutes, and write down your thoughts now. Do this every morning and every evening, if possible. If morning does not work, use your coffee break at midmorning. See how much clearer and grounded you start to feel. You are creating a clear channel for new memory, new thoughts, and new focus.

INTENTION:

Our deepest intentions are carried not only in our minds but are felt throughout our bodies. Intentions are powerful, and the intention with which we do something is directly related to the result or outcome that we produce. For example, if I give money to a person or an organization to affect change or support some cause close to my heart, the money is being used for good. It is a very different intention if I give the money solely for my name to be used on something, or if I am just giving it so others will think I am a generous person. In the latter circumstances, the ego is controlling the intention. It can be a very positive thing for someone's name to be used on something, but it is all in the intention. When the ego is in control, it will not generate the same result for the person. It is important to think about your intention before taking an action. The more we focus on an intention, the more powerful it becomes.

Some intentions are small and some are larger. As you set small intentions each day, you will feel your focus and energy start to shift as you have an inner knowing that as you go through your day, you are aligning yourself with a universal power in every action that you take. For example, if I set an intention to do the best job I can at work each day, I can focus my efforts knowing that my intention is supported by the universe, God, the quantum field, all responding to me, helping me to do this fantastic job. Think of the power in that intention! Intentions that are more complicated may take more time, as pieces may have to be put into place for that particular situation to manifest itself.

When an intention is written clearly, over and over, the solution starts to present itself as the mind is trained to focus on finding a solution. In Deepak Chopra's book *Ageless Body, Timeless Mind*, he states that "An intention is a signal sent from you to the field, and the result you get back from the field is the highest fulfillment that can be delivered to your particular nervous system."[16] Intention is one of the most powerful tools we have at our disposal. It is a conscious focus that starts a chain of events beginning in our brain with the reprogramming of our own neural pathways and connecting us with the greater quantum field. Repetition is an important part of reprogramming our brain, which is why writing our intentions over and over is important.

When writing an intention, it is important to think about the following things:

- Write the intention with clarity.
- Be specific about what you want, including as much detail as possible.
- Expect results.
- Keep track of your results.
- Think of other times in your life when you have gotten results.
- "Let go," knowing the highest fulfillment possible is in motion.

3. Write an intention now. Be as focused and detailed as possible.

4. Visualize and feel what it will be like when your intention manifests itself. Remember, your subconscious is programmed through your sensory system. Close your eyes, and feel the sensations.

5. Rewrite your intention every day until you see results of some kind.

6. Journal/write about the results you got from your intention. If it was not the full result you wanted, search your mind for the block or barrier to that intention. Write about that.

7. Write a small intention each day. Example: I intend to be loving to everyone I meet today.

8. Journal/write what happens in response to the small intentions you write and set each day. You will be amazed at the opportunities that appear to support your small intention and the shifts that take place around you.

9. Write to your Muse:
   Journal/write to your Muse fifteen to thirty minutes each day. Ask your Muse for guidance to help you to be clear about what you want in your life and in describing your intentions. Write about what your life will be like when your intentions manifest themselves.

Benefit Five:
Creativity

I USED TO DO A WORKSHOP CALLED "IS THE UNKNOWN BECKONING YOU?" THE "UNKNOWN" IS THE GAP, THE VOID, THE PLACE WHERE WE ALL MUST GO TO TAKE THE NEXT STEP OR FIND OUR CREATIVE SPIRIT. WHEN WE ARE OPERATING OFF OF INFORMATION WE ALREADY KNOW, WE ARE ACCESSING THE SUBCONSCIOUS. WHEN WE HAVE AN IDEA, OR A CREATIVE, IMAGINATIVE THOUGHT, WE ARE LISTENING TO THE CONSCIOUS. AS WE OBSERVE NATURE, WE REALIZE IT IS EVER CHANGING AND IN CONSTANT CREATION. WE WERE BORN TO LIVE IN CYCLES AND CHANGE, LIKE NATURE. ONE CYCLE ENDS AND ANOTHER BEGINS ... THE UNKNOWN IS THE GAP THAT WE ENTER BETWEEN THE CYCLES OF OUR LIVES. OUR PAST IS BEHIND US, AND THE FUTURE PATH IS NOT YET FORMED. IT IS ALSO THE PLACE WHERE WE DIVE INTO THE COSMOS, THE CONSCIOUS CREATIVE AND IMAGINATIVE SPIRIT, WHERE IDEAS SPARK AND IMAGINATION EXPLODES.

Touching our creative spirit ignites the passion in us. When people describe what they love to do, it is usually something that feels very natural to them. They often say, "It doesn't feel like work, it feels natural." I had another great insight on my trip to Morocco. I was struck by the way the people of that country use everything, and it all comes from the land—it's natural. They are working with the land, not against it. The dyes for the shoes, the leather, the oils, the food, the list goes on and on; it all comes from the land. Many of the men and women of Morocco are artisans or people with a distinguished craft that has been handed down in their particular family for generations. One man created stonework art pieces from the imaginative patterns he designed in his head. Piece after piece, all the small, brightly colored stones and patterns were crafted carefully together; no two were the same. He had done that for forty years, which I find simply amazing. What is natural to you—what is your true nature? What speaks to you in the silence like nothing else?

Many people have a tendency to work against what is natural to them and feel frustrated and worn out because they cannot succeed or excel. Where is the place that you excel, and it feels normal? That special place is where it feels natural to expand, where you feel alive inside and dare to go beyond your limits. The ebb and flow of the tides of the ocean is a natural process. It is a part of God's perfect plan, each wave creating a new design in the sand. Some waves reach higher and farther than others, all a part of the plan. The natural expansion and contraction of the ocean, like our breath, helps us connect to the magnificent rhythm of the universe, the creative forces vibrating in each of us.

As we write the story of our path, we explore what feels natural to us. In this natural, creative state, we observe ourselves expanding and contracting. The natural expansion feels like flight, as we extend our wings and go beyond the ordinary. We are not sure where this flight is taking us, but something resonates inside, and we feel the natural rhythm. This expansion doesn't feel hard; it feels exciting, exhilarating. When we contract, we pull back, into our shells, contemplating and grounding our being, assimilating our new experiences in order to take off again and soar to a place we have never been.

As we heighten the awareness of our thoughts, we are reminded again that the right brain sees the big picture filled with thoughts, emotions, and psychological responses. For this conceptual thinking and new thoughts to emerge, we must have space for that to happen. To explore our own creativity, we have to create the space, a place where we can simply think, try new things, or pull all the pieces together.

Journaling helps us learn to express ourselves. As we journal and tap into our expressive powers, it ignites the creative spark within. As you begin the exercises below, think about ways you can create some space for growth and exploration to nurture the creative part of your life. Sometimes growth makes us feel anxious—that's okay, you're growing! Enjoy the process!

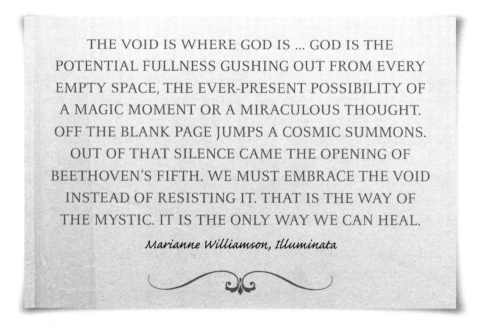

THE VOID IS WHERE GOD IS … GOD IS THE POTENTIAL FULLNESS GUSHING OUT FROM EVERY EMPTY SPACE, THE EVER-PRESENT POSSIBILITY OF A MAGIC MOMENT OR A MIRACULOUS THOUGHT. OFF THE BLANK PAGE JUMPS A COSMIC SUMMONS. OUT OF THAT SILENCE CAME THE OPENING OF BEETHOVEN'S FIFTH. WE MUST EMBRACE THE VOID INSTEAD OF RESISTING IT. THAT IS THE WAY OF THE MYSTIC. IT IS THE ONLY WAY WE CAN HEAL.

Marianne Williamson, Illuminata

We are all unique, and discovering our own unique qualities is an important tool when trying to understand how to use our talents and abilities. Each part of the brain has unique traits, and we all have abilities from both the right and left brain spheres. Some individuals have developed certain parts of their brain more than others. The right hemisphere is known for holding the limbic system, which processes the streams of information that burst into our brain via the sensory system. The right brain works well at synthesizing information and perceiving things as a whole.

Exercises: Creativity

1. *Close your eyes and ... Breathe, ... again, ... again, ... again!*

2. When have you expanded yourself beyond what was ordinary or familiar? Write and describe that place.

3. How did that feel? Journal/write about that feeling.

4. What have you done in your life that feels the most natural to you; specifically, what calls you and makes you feel connected to your own rhythm, your own passion? Write and describe what that was and what it felt like.

5. Would you be willing to do that again? If yes, why? If no, why not?

6. What could you possibly change to allow you to explore that again? Explain.

7. How do you make yourself feel grounded? What does that feel like? Describe.

8. List some things that make you feel grounded.

9. When have you felt yourself in a "flow"? Journal/write about that time.

10. Start to observe the synchronicity in your life. Journal/write about those moments.

11. Make a plan for the next week. As you write your plan, include things in your plan that do the following:

    • Create silence, such as meditation or prayer.

    • Have one new experience, even if it is just driving to work a different way.

    • Spend some time outdoors, in nature.

    • Do one thing for yourself—yoga, an art class, Nia dance—where you can express yourself in a different way.

    • Make a creative object for someone you care about, a card, a picture.

- Journal/write about how you feel in these new experiences.
- Make a mandala.

12. Where is the place in your life where you express your creativity?

13. When have you had the opportunity to assimilate different pieces of your own life/career together and use them in new ways? Write about that.

14. Conceptual thinking is the ability to "see the big picture." When have you had that experience? In a career, personal life, relationship? Write about that.

Intuition

Intuition is a matter of honoring the still, small voice inside of us that says, "Do this!" "Don't do that!" We can teach ourselves to use our intuition by being quiet and listening. It is hard to do that when cognitive reasoning is the voice that usually steers us around. Intuition is pure energy. When you receive an intuitive message, resist the urge to figure out what it means. Do not try to overdetermine the significance. Receive the information through the senses and just sit with it, knowing the outcome will be revealed to you. If you have an intuition that you absolutely should not do something, listen to that message.

15. When have you had an intuitive thought or received an intuitive message? Describe that situation.

16. The more you use your intuition, the more it will be available to you. This week, write each day about listening to your intuition, and what happened. As you test out your intuition, have fun with it!

Imagination

I can remember lying in the front yard as a child, looking at the clouds, and making up stories in my head. That is exactly what imagination is, creating pictures in our minds out of images of all the possibilities we can imagine. Imagination has no limits. Every successful business or idea draws from someone's imaginative process.

As children, we daydream. As we get older and go through school, we have all heard the warning, "Stop daydreaming!" The reverse should actually be true. We should give awards for the best daydream. The great gift of imagination comes out of our conscious. To really explore the creative parts of ourselves, we have to enter the field of all possibility where our imagination can "play" with all the ideas that are not just possible, but impossible—the ideas that haven't been created yet. Allow your mind to create new neurons that explore your imagination. Enjoy!

17. When was the last time you daydreamed? Journal/write about your memory of that.

18. Schedule a time with yourself to let your imagination run free. Describe what you thought about. Don't feel guilty!

19. If you could imagine yourself doing anything, what would that be? Journal/write the details of that. Expand on this every day.

20. Think about what you wrote in the previous question. How do you see this fitting into the bigger picture of the world? Write about that.

21. Journal/write to your Muse: write to your Muse for fifteen to thirty minutes each day. Ask your Muse to help you create a special place or time to explore your creative nature. Journal/write about how you might do that.

Benefit Six:
Authenticity

AS WE PEEL BACK THE LAYERS UNCOVERING THE DIFFERENT PARTS OF OURSELVES, WE ARE BEGINNING TO GET AN IDEA OF WHO WE WERE CREATED TO BE. AS WE LET GO OF CERTAIN THINGS IN OUR LIVES, IT IS NOT ALWAYS EASY. THE PARTS WE ARE LETTING GO OF ARE LIKE FAMILIAR FRIENDS. IT MAKES US ACKNOWLEDGE THAT WE ARE CHANGING, AND SOME THINGS MUST BE LEFT BEHIND. LETTING GO IS NOT FORGETTING. WE HOLD THOSE PEOPLE AND THINGS WE LOVE FOREVER IN OUR HEADS AND HEARTS. LETTING GO IS A PROCESS AND A SERIES OF SMALL STEPS. AS WE UNDERSTAND HOW TO CONTAIN OUR MEMORY IN A NEW WAY, WE CAN ALLOW A HIGHER SPIRIT TO HELP US LET GO AND RELEASE OUR GRIP ON THE PAST, ENABLING US TO BE CARRIED FORWARD WITHOUT RESISTANCE. THE MEMORY IS A PART OF OUR EXPERIENCE OF WHO WE ARE. LETTING GO IS AN ESSENTIAL STEP TO BECOMING OUR AUTHENTIC SELVES, AS WE CAN NO LONGER CARRY ALL THE LABELS, EXPECTATIONS, AND CLUTTER IN OUR BACKPACK. IT'S JUST TOO HEAVY.

Congruent is one of my favorite words. The word congruent describes someone who is the same on the outside as they are on the inside. If I am congruent, my actions reflect who I really am. If you have been doing the exercises in this book, you have begun to peel back the layers of things that no longer describe who you are, to discover the authentic self. But, the self is not just contained in the body ... it is a combination of the body, the mind, and the spirit. As you assimilate your experiences, each part of the self has an impact on the other.

Think of the people you are most attracted to. Why are you attracted to them? We are not attracted to people because of their looks—we are attracted to people because they are fully present, willing to be engaged, and we can connect with them. Many people are attracted to the Dalai Lama. Why are people so attracted to him? They are attracted because they can connect with him. Being authentic requires you to allow yourself to have passion and not be ashamed of it—regardless of what someone else might think.

Why are you attracted to certain movies? What happened? How did you connect so strongly? You connected to the emotion of the actor, you connected to the character—to the humanity of that character. Many times we do not allow ourselves to be "all of who we are" because of what other people might think, or, in actuality, we do not really know who we are! But, sometimes we see it in someone else, and it gives us a glimpse of a part of our self. It resonates within our whole being.

I work part time at a clinic for chronically ill young adults. When Dr. P. walks into the room, she looks at Johnny, who is sitting in his wheelchair, with his arms and hands curled up from muscle spasms and his head to one side, as a result of his disease, cerebral palsy. She puts her hand on his shoulder, looks directly into his eyes, and, with a bright smile, asks how he is doing. She doesn't treat him like he is abnormal or doesn't exist. She directs her questions to him, and allows him to answer, even though it might take a long time or not happen at all. She is fully present to Johnny. She is passionate about Johnny and the hundreds of other "Johnnys" in her life. People love to work with Dr. P. Why? They are drawn to her because she is authentic. She is not afraid to show up and be present in any situation. Her ego doesn't come into the room ahead of her. Johnny feels like he is as important to Dr. P. as the other doctors in the room.

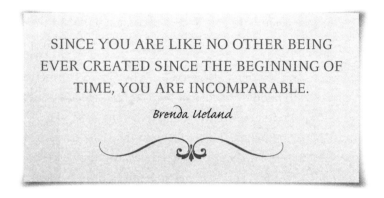

SINCE YOU ARE LIKE NO OTHER BEING EVER CREATED SINCE THE BEGINNING OF TIME, YOU ARE INCOMPARABLE.

Brenda Ueland

Sometimes we have to go through a period of not knowing who we are in order to reassemble the pieces, to find out who we are becoming. After the death of my husband Tom, I went through a period of not knowing who I was at all. The person I thought I was supposed to be simply didn't exist anymore. It took a few years of searching before I really understood who this new person was that was emerging from that old skin. Like alchemy, we are redefined by the layers that are peeled off to find the gold, or the authentic self, inside of us. Are we ever finished? No; each experience gives us an opportunity to be present and continue to peel, and find more gold.

Exercises: The Authentic Self

1. *Close your eyes and ... Breathe, ... again, ... again, ... again!*

2. What is the persona or personas of whom you think you "should" be? This could be cultural, family beliefs, etc. Journal/write about that persona or personas, and when you can let that persona go and when you cannot.

3. For one day, monitor yourself. Try being present in every situation you encounter. It takes a lot of work! Write about your experience of being

present and how different it feels.

4. As you allow yourself to "be yourself," what do you have to let go of? We have emotional clutter and physical clutter. What is the clutter in your life that keeps you stuck and that you need to let go of? (Clutter can be a title, stuff, way of life, or a barrier of any kind.) Write about that.

5. As you redesign your life, what are the components that make you feel resourceful and effective and reflect the person you are becoming?

Ego

Have you ever had the experience of looking back over a period in your life and said, "Who was that person!" A friend of mine was going through his boxes in his garage trying to decide what to keep and what to get rid of—probably something we can all relate to. As he looked through boxes of trophies and pictures of himself receiving awards, he said, "Who was that guy?" He had gone through a period in his life when he was completely out of balance and overidentified with his career and image in the community. His ego was fully in charge. He acknowledged that he probably really never "showed up," because when he did, it was all about his current title or the award. Fortunately, he could now clearly look back and see that person.

This is a great story about the ego. We need the ego to have an identity and define who we are in our lives. But, when the ego is "in charge," the balance shifts, and we confine ourselves to exist within the boxes the ego creates. The ego *loves* to be stroked, encourages separation, judges others, and always wants to have the answer—to be right.

Carl was a man who had gone to Harvard and was an executive with a large company. Carl wanted to support nonprofits in the world, so he decided to quit his executive position and started creating nonprofits in third-world countries. Fortunately for Carl, money was not the issue. All of a sudden, however, he didn't have a business card. He didn't have any of the titles or a place to go every day. Carl said that it was one of the hardest times in his life. At first, he felt depression, anxiety, and regret about his decision, based on a passion he had felt so drawn to. What happened? The ego went crazy! The ego sent the great message—you are worthless because you are no longer a ... name a category.

Slowly, Carl started to redefine his purpose and listen to the wisdom within to understand why he was so drawn to nonprofit work. As he went inward and became clear and defined about his purpose, everything started to change. Carl is one of the most authentic, energetic, and attractive people I know—who does incredible, amazing work in the small villages of the world.

It is important to think about our balance, and to monitor our ego. For example, when I give workshops, I have to monitor my ego. I have to remind myself that I am the messenger, and I am fortunate to be able to do this work in the world. It's not about me. If we can monitor the ego, we can use it to help us, not to control our actions and prevent us from becoming who we were created to be.

6. How has your ego affected you in the past? Journal/write about that person.

7. Think about when your ego affects you the most. Describe that person.

8. How can you become more aware of monitoring the ego?

GURUS CAN TEACH US SKILLS AND TECHNIQUES.
THEY CAN INCREASE YOUR UNDERSTANDINGS
OF LIFE, DEATH AND THE SPIRITUAL PLANES.
THEY CAN HELP REMOVE FEARS AND OBSTACLES.
THEY CAN POINT OUT THE DOORWAY,
BUT IT IS WE WHO MUST GO THROUGH THE DOOR.

Messages from the Masters

9. Image yourself as a baby, before you had an ego. Think of all the gifts and potential that existed within this small child. Journal/write about who this child was created to be. This is a powerful exercise. Take your time writing this.

10. Journal/write to your Muse: write for fifteen to thirty minutes each day.

   For the next week, ask your Muse to point out when the ego is in control. Ask your Muse to help you become more aware of this. Write about when your ego was in charge this week. This may surprise you! Learn to laugh at your ego.

Benefit Seven:
Vision and Dreams

WE ALL HAVE A DREAM. WITHOUT OUR CREATIVE
IMAGINATION, PASSION, AND WISDOM, WE WOULD NOT
HAVE A DREAM. OUT OF OUR DREAMS COMES OUR VISION. MANY
OF US FEEL WE CANNOT ACCOMPLISH OUR DREAM BECAUSE IT
IS TOO BIG OR OUT OF OUR REACH. SO MANY DREAMS BECOME
DEFEATED BEFORE THEY GET STARTED. MANY PEOPLE DO NOT
TALK ABOUT THEIR DREAMS BECAUSE THEY THINK THEIR DREAMS
CANNOT HAPPEN. LIKE ANYTHING ELSE, DREAMS HAVE TO BE
BROKEN DOWN INTO DIGESTIBLE BITES. AS WE START TO INITIATE
THE SMALL BABY STEPS OF OUR DREAM, IT IS LIKE PUTTING OUR
TOE IN THE WATER; WE ARE TESTING THE WATER. STARTING SLOW
WE CAN WATCH THE DREAM UNFOLD INTO A VISION AND BECOME
A REALITY. LIKE ANYTHING THAT GROWS, IT IS A PROCESS AND
HAPPENS ONE STEP AT A TIME. WE HAVE TO BE WILLING TO WALK,
NOT RUN, TOWARD OUR NEW VISION.

I am fortunate that in the work I do to hear a lot of really great stories, and
Mike's story was no exception. I recently received a call from a friend who
wanted me to meet Mike for breakfast. Even though the business sector has

started to explore journaling as a tool for creative and conceptual thinking, I was curious why someone like Mike, a very successful businessman, would be interested in the work that I do. He began the discussion saying that he was interested in journaling and how that worked, and he wanted to tell me his story and experience with journaling. Mike proceeded to tell me that in 2000, he owned a company that provided outsourcing services for information technology. His company had made a lot of money by anyone's standards. As outsourcing in the market took a downturn, his business began to struggle. Accounts declined, and he was letting people go. In fact, it was so bad that he was looking at filing for bankruptcy. He could not even pay his phone bill. He was going to have to go to his board and tell them the bad news.

He found that he was spending more and more time at home, and, as he put it, "under the covers." It was too painful to go to the office. Fortunately, he had a wonderful wife who would not let him stay at home and mope. She gently told him he had to "get it together" and do something. So instead of lying in bed every day, as he was tempted to do, he started going to Starbucks across the street from his office every morning and journaling. It was better than being at the office where all of the creditors were calling. At first, he wrote about how awful things were and that he saw no solutions. He wrote about his fears and all the terrible things that could happen, and were happening.

Then, after several weeks, his writing started to change. He started writing about a new vision for a company he wanted to create. He did not know exactly what the company would do, but he had several goals. He wanted a company that did something no other company in the world did. He wanted to work with people with integrity and offer great services. He continued to refine his vision of what he wanted, adding more and more details. He went to Starbucks every day and journaled, pouring out his creative passion onto the pages, focusing on the new vision.

After several weeks, just as he was about to have to let everything in his company go, he got a call. It was from a major computer company. It wanted to hire a team of people to come into the company and do a set of specific tasks and then leave. It was not the way management had conducted business before, but they wanted to try a new model. It was the first job for the "new company" that Mike had been envisioning. From that job, he started to pay off his creditors and got completely out of debt. Now he sends teams all over the world to do the same thing. His company makes more money than his first company did, which was part of his vision. Since that time, Mike has journaled about many other goals that have later become realities in his life.

As I listened to his story, I helped him put the pieces together to understand what was happening in his brain as his thoughts flowed on to the pages every morning. As Mike journaled, he went through the process of identifying and downloading his losses, fears, and the turmoil that was bombarding his thoughts and his body. He identified his losses and acknowledged mistakes. As he cleared his mind and his body, he could actually think about what he had left and reframe that into thoughts about a new company. As he wrote, he acknowledged the positive things about his old company, but he described in vivid detail what he envisioned in his new company. The daily, repetitive, new thoughts created new neural connections and pictures. Our brain is designed to bring us what we program into the subconscious. It brought Mike exactly what he had envisioned. Repetition is the key for the brain, and he did this every day!

Remember the NASA experiment in the first chapter? New data was put into the brain, and it built a new neural pathway. Reprogramming the subconscious takes a lot of repetition and clarity. Without realizing it, that is exactly what Mike did. Journaling is a full-body experience which activates the sensory and creates vivid pictures in our minds. When we change our thoughts, our beliefs change, our body chemistry changes, our actions change, and our life changes.

Exercises: Vision and Dreams

1. *Close your eyes and ... Breathe, ... again, ... again, ... again!*

2. Journal/write about any preoccupation that is repeating itself in your mind. Write about it every day for fifteen to thirty minutes to help clear the

repetitive thoughts. This may take several days every week for a while.

3. Journal about how you would like your life to be. As you redefine yourself, include the following:

    • Where you would like to live (mountains, city, etc.)
    • The lifestyle you would like to have (travel, exercise, etc.)
    • The type of work you would like to have and the schedule
    • The people you would like to be with
    • Identify your passion! (You may have already done this in the Creativity section)
    • Define your purpose or some components of what that might be
    • Spiritual beliefs
    • Financial goals

    Journal/write about this as if it were happening now. Create a vivid, written picture.

4. Think of another time in your life when you were really happy, joyful, and passionate. Include the skills you mastered at that time and all aspects of the situation. Feel it throughout your body. Write about this time.

5. Focus on one aspect of what you wrote in question 3 that you do not currently have in your life. Identify all the parts of that. For example, the type of work. Journal and describe in detail what you want that part of your life to look like. Repetition is the key. Write about this every day.

6. Visualize what having that "one thing" would feel like. This should be similar to the feeling you had in question 4. Do this several times a day along with your journaling. Write about the key concepts of this part of your vision. Keep them on a piece of paper and keep them with you. Focus on them every day.

7. Create a poster that reflects your new lifestyle. Keep it where you can see it and look at it every day.

Purpose:

This question seems to be on everyone's mind these days. What is your "purpose" on the planet? Purpose does not have to be complicated; it can be as simple as "helping others." It is important to identify our purpose in order to have a vision that fits our purpose. The following is an exercise that has proven useful to many who are trying to define their purpose.

8. Make a list of everything you have done in your life. Work, home, relationships, family, church activities, social activities—all of it. After you list all the things you have done, look for the common thread that runs through each thing. There is always a thread. You just have to find it. It will show itself to you. When you find the thread, write down the words that describe it. That is your purpose. Your purpose can manifest itself in many ways. Your vision may change throughout your life; your purpose will not. Write about the various ways your purpose has manifested itself in your life.

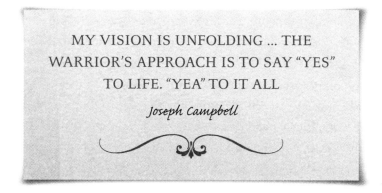

MY VISION IS UNFOLDING ... THE WARRIOR'S APPROACH IS TO SAY "YES" TO LIFE. "YEA" TO IT ALL

Joseph Campbell

Vision:

Vision statements vary at different times in your life. Some of my clients have gotten stuck thinking that what they write will never be able to change. A vision statement does not have to be complicated. If you are writing a personal vision statement, it may include your purpose and the way you want to affect people's lives at this time. The same is true with a business. As a business grows, the vision will change as it expands.

A vision statement is a broad statement that should include the following:

- Your purpose and passion;
- Your concept of how you are going to express that vision in the world.
- The statement should be short, only a few sentences.
- It should be written in the now, not in the future.

9. Journal/write about everything you would like to include in your vision statement. Include your purpose in your vision.

    Example: My purpose is to help others find joy. Vision: my vision is to help others find joy by taking beautiful pictures for everyone in the world to see.

10. Write a personal vision statement for yourself. Your personal vision should include things you are passionate about and what you think your purpose is on the planet. Keep this statement with you, in your pocket. Carry it around. Put it in your office, or on your computer, where you can see it. It will guide everything in your life toward your vision.

11. Identify some small steps you can take toward realizing your vision.

12. Make a vision board with pictures that reflect your vision.

13. Write to your Muse: journal/write to your Muse fifteen to thirty minutes each day.

    Write a question to your Muse before you go to bed about something you are not clear about in your future. Ask your Muse to provide the answer. Keep your journal beside your bed in case the answer comes in the form of a dream.

PART THREE

Journaling Through:
At Work

Benefit One:
Health and Wellness at Work

Health and Wellness at Work
- Reduces absenteeism
- Reduces illness
- Fewer physician visits

*I*N OUR BUSY LIVES, JOURNALING BRINGS US ANOTHER TOOL TO SUPPORT OUR IMMUNE SYSTEM AND ENHANCE OUR MENTAL HEALTH. OUR HEALTH IS ESSENTIAL TO MAINTAIN IN ORDER FOR US AS INDIVIDUALS TO BE ABLE TO FOCUS ON RELEASING THE CREATIVE RESERVES OF ENERGY THAT WE NEED TO BRING INTO THE WORKPLACE.

This is evidenced by many of the clients whom I see in my practice. Typically when people have experienced something in their personal lives that is unresolved, it affects every other part of their life, especially their health. Most issues that confront individuals are not resolved in a day, or even a few weeks.

One client, after experiencing a divorce, started to have anxiety attacks and suffered sleep disruption. He felt his ability to function and make decisions were greatly affected. His expectation was that he should just "get over it" and move on. He did not want to burden his friends, or appear weak and vulnerable at work. He had buried every emotion he felt from the divorce, and it was now causing physical symptoms. Rather than attend therapy weekly, he wanted a tool that he could use on his own and access therapy when he needed it. I started him on the journaling exercises and questions. It gave him the chance to explore his feelings and acknowledge the enormous loss that he had experienced. As a result of the journaling, his anxiety lessened, and he was able to start to refocus his efforts on work. Journaling in the evening helped his sleep pattern to improve, as well as his mood.

Questionnaire studies with two hundred corporate employees found that having at least one significant trauma in their lives which they chose not to discuss was related to heightened incidence of both major and minor health problems, including cancer and hypertension, and colds and flu, respectively.[17] In studies with college students, investigators found that individuals who were randomly assigned to write about personally upsetting topics for three to five consecutive days evidenced fewer physician visits than subjects who wrote about superficial topics.[18]

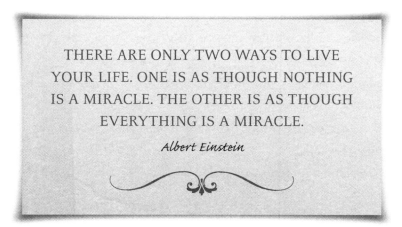

THERE ARE ONLY TWO WAYS TO LIVE YOUR LIFE. ONE IS AS THOUGH NOTHING IS A MIRACLE. THE OTHER IS AS THOUGH EVERYTHING IS A MIRACLE.

Albert Einstein

Postexperimental questionnaires from the disclosure studies by Pennebaker indicated that putting upsetting events into words changed how participants dealt with past events and ongoing life circumstances.[19] Various disclosure studies have indicated that encouraging individuals to write or talk about personal upheavals is associated not only with improved physical health, but also reduced absentee rates among employed adults,[20] and better classroom performance and long-term elevations in life satisfaction among college students.[21]

Understanding this information gives us a framework in which to explore the exercises as a useful tool for the workplace in order to process and contain specific, stressful situations in our lives. Remember, the exercises are a guide to help you begin the journaling process and can be done multiple times for various situations. In our busy lives, journaling brings us another tool to support our immune systems and enhance our physical and mental health.

Exercises: Health Benefits

1. *Close your eyes and ... Breathe, ... again, ... again, ... again!*

2. Become aware of your body. We all have many situations that give us stress. Think about one stressful situation that you are dealing with now. How does your body feel? Where are you carrying your stress? This is your body's reaction to this stress. Journal/write how your body *feels* when you think about the situation or a particular aspect of that situation that gives you stress.

3. Write about the stressful situation. Describe it as if you were talking to someone.

4. What are the blocks in your path that are preventing you from solving this stressful situation? Journal/write about the blocks.

5. You are standing in your future looking back on the year. As you look back, what do you see clearly that you wish you had done differently about this stressful situation? Describe that.

6. Now, think about the blocks you wrote about in question 4 that are keeping you from moving through this stressful situation. Now that you have a picture of what you wish you had done differently, how could you work with the blocks differently than you are now? All movement begins

with small steps. What small steps can you make now? Write about these small steps.

7. Ideally, how would you like to see the situation resolved? Journal/write about that.

To move forward to make things happen differently, I am going to move you mentally to a different place ... Are you ready? Let your new thoughts start bubbling ...

When was the last time your body felt free, alive, energized? When you were a child? Adult? Bring up this memory and write about it now. As you write about this memory, think about the positive, good chemicals cascading to all the cells throughout your body.

8. Think about this memory every day. You want to reactivate the chemicals connected to this memory and all of the good feelings and mental pictures that go with this memory. Wow! Journal about this memory again.

9. What could give you this same feeling in the present? Write about a situation that could be possible, which you would like to see happen, that would give you those same good feelings. Write about this as often as you can, every day if possible. It is important to be clear and specific, and keep expanding the idea as you journal. As you journal, construct mental pictures to reflect this situation.

10. Cut out some pictures that represent this happy, past feeling and your new, desired situation that would help you reexperience this feeling in the present. Put them on a board, or make a screensaver of these pictures where you can see them every day. As you repeat the images, you are filling your body and cells with new, powerful, positive chemicals and brain reinforcement.

11. Journal/write about how you would be different if what you want manifested itself, and you felt this way every day.

12. Write to your Muse.

The word *muse* is taken from Greek mythology. Ancient Roman or Greek writers would often begin their poems by asking for the aid of the Muses in their competitions. The word *muse* means "to inspire." The Muse helps us tell our own story. So, take the time to journal to your Muse for at least fifteen to thirty minutes every day. Ask your Muse the most important question that is stirring in your mind. Your Muse may take the form of God, Spirit, Higher Self, Jesus, Buddha, or some other guide. Expect to get an answer.

Benefit Two:
Awareness at Work

Awareness at Work
- Improves problem-solving skills
- Synergistic effect—unites people as a team

AWARENESS AND PERCEPTION OF OUR OWN THOUGHTS HELP TO IDENTIFY REPETITIVE PATTERNS. AS AWARENESS IS HEIGHTENED, AN INDIVIDUAL LEARNS TO RECOGNIZE THE BARRIERS AND BELIEFS THAT EXIST. THESE BARRIERS CAN BE FROM A LOSS OR WOUND THAT HAS NOT BEEN HEALED, AND SO THESE BARRIERS HAVE NOT BEEN BROUGHT INTO OUR FIELD OF AWARENESS.

In the work setting, it is important to be able to consider all possibilities to have a synergistic approach. Teamwork requires this type of synergy. The application of awareness can open an individual to the possibility of shifting a perception to enable that person to explore another's point of view. Rather than reacting, we learn to respond—an important problem-solving skill.

A recent client situation demonstrated this principle. Lisa came to me to discuss the difficulty she was having in relationships in her personal life and at work. She had recently moved away from friends and family. She had always had a lot of support and now felt as though she had to prove herself to all of the new people she was meeting. In addition, she had been a decision maker at her last job, and she felt that no one appreciated that experience or listened to her. In meetings, she would shut down, feeling like she was "not heard," and became defensive and angry as a result.

As Lisa explored her story through the awareness exercises and journaling, she became aware of her enormous losses and the grief that held her emotions captive and kept her from moving forward. Moving had left Lisa separated from everyone to whom she was connected and close. Her support system had vanished. The loss was a lot bigger for Lisa than she had realized. Identifying her own patterns and finding containment for her losses enabled Lisa to interact differently with her peers in her personal life and at work. She began to engage again at meetings and exhibit the strengths that were true to her nature.

In studies by Pennebaker, it was found that disclosing and writing about certain traumatic information, and finding closure, aids in general problem-solving skills. The ability to work through negative feelings, to assimilate and attain closure on loss and achieve a new perspective, is an important skill.[22]

As you focus on the questions in the exercises pertaining to awareness, know that the process of journaling is providing you with a new tool to enhance your problem-solving abilities and perceptions.

Exercises: Awareness

1. *Close your eyes and ... Breathe, ... again, ... again, ... again!*
2. Write down a situation that you are struggling with, or that you want to change that makes you unhappy or discontent. This might be a relationship, your job and/or career, finances, family situation, living situation, or other.
3. How long have you struggled with this situation? Explain.
4. What is your "story" about this situation, and why it is the way it is, or

can't change? Journal/write about that.

5. What are the *unconscious* thoughts or "rote" tapes that feed my discontentment that continue in my head and feed my "story" when I think about this situation? Journal/write these down.

6. What patterns do you see in this situation that remind you of a pattern in your family? Write down these patterns. Remember, thoughts trigger other thoughts. You may think of more to journal about.

7. Every time I think about this situation I feel _____ (angry, misunderstood, anxious, depressed, unhappy, victimized, stuck, or other).

8. Is there a way to look at this situation differently? Remember, we can't change another person, but we can change the way we look at things. What is a new, *conscious* way you could look at this situation? A conscious thought aligns you with the present. In other words, use new words to describe the old story.

    Write a new, *conscious* thought that could describe the situation differently, and change the story.

    Journal/write the new story as you would like it to be.

LOSS:
Most of us have experienced a loss or multiple losses in our lives. As you explore the losses in your life, remember a loss can be a career, job, divorce, relationship, death, move, or illness. One loss can trigger other losses.

9. Identify your losses. Write a list of the losses in your life.

10. Identify the biggest or most important loss you have experienced. What feelings does the change or loss bring up for you? (Fear, vulnerability, anger, etc.) Journal/write about these feelings now.

11. Is there a loss you are still preoccupied with? What is the preoccupation in your head?

12. Name some of the losses or changes you have navigated in the past. We all have strengths to get through things. Write about how you handled these losses and what strengths you used to get through these losses.

13. The past can only be healed in the present. Journal/write about how it feels to be here now, even if it's difficult.

14. Journal/write about how you can take care of yourself while dealing with this loss.

15. The loss is *part* of your identity, but not *all* of your identity. Journal/write about how you can move forward in your life, incorporating the loss.

DECISIONS:

Contemplate decisions which have been made in your life. There have been major decisions in your life that defined you. These are turning points in your path that led you in a specific direction. Some of these decisions may have seemed right, others may have led to important lessons, and other decisions you may regret.

16. What decisions were made *for you* that have helped define you?

17. What decisions did *you make* that have helped define you?

18. Which decisions have impacted your identity, "who you are," the most?

IDENTITY:

Who am I? Not a simple question. If our cells are regenerating themselves every day, I am not the same person today as I was three years ago, or even last year! Science has shown that we continue development throughout our adult lives as our brains continue to change. As you have more and more experiences, you change with each experience. Decisions impact our identity. Identity builds. It is important to reflect on certain parts of ourselves that we value and treasure, as well as identify new parts of ourselves that are growing. Keep this in mind as you reflect on the question of identity.

19. Identity: How would you describe your identity five years ago, ten years

ago? Journal/write about that person.

20. What situations have made you change or redefine your identity? What does your new identity look like now? What are the important parts of your old identity that you have kept? Journal/write about that new identity now.

What drives our behavior?

As we explore our motivation for doing something, that process can shift our awareness to become more conscious of our actions, and we can use our actions to benefit ourselves and others. We can be driven by both positive and negative emotions, which affect the outcome of what we do. Also, the degree to which something drives us is important.

For example: If I am driven by fear, a little fear could motivate me to do better; or, if taken too far, fear could cause me to steal, lie, or compromise my integrity in other negative ways.

21. What drives your behavior? Fear, loss, depression, perfection, love, helping others, money, other? Identifying what drives our behavior helps us understand and become more conscious of our actions, and if they are coming from a positive place or a negative place.
    a) Write about what drives your life, your behavior.
    b) Write about what happens when you allow yourself to be driven too far. Journal/write about what you can do to manage your behavior before it goes further than you want it to.

What touches our wounds or triggers our behavior?

We all have wounds. Wounds are sensitive places that lie within each of us. If a wound is not yet healed, someone else's actions or words can trigger our wound, causing a strong reaction in us; when someone says or does something that touches that sensitive place, we react. Certain situations can cause strong emotions and reactions in us. In order to heal a wound, it is important to look at the feelings it brings up in us. Self-awareness of when we feel vulnerable or have strong emotional reactions to a situation helps us to be mindful of our wounds that need healing.

On a good day, we can keep our emotions in check, and on a not-so-good day, we cannot. As we explore who we really are, we need to understand what touches or opens our wounds. Becoming aware of what triggers our behavior, or provokes a strong emotion in us, helps us to monitor how we choose to react, and move forward to heal.

22. What triggers or elicits a strong emotion in you? Old wounds, losses, beliefs, fear, control, other? Identifying when you have a strong reaction to someone else will give you an awareness and insight into the wounds in you that need to heal. If people are walking on eggshells around you, it is possible you are getting triggered very easily. Awareness of our own responses to things and situations that provoke us or elicit a strong reaction is key to changing our own behavior or acknowledging the wounds that need to heal.

    Journal/write about what triggers your behavior or causes a strong emotional reaction in you, and what you can do to manage yourself. Can you identify the wound that this touches in you? Write about that.

23. What are the Ahas you have discovered? Write a list of these.

24. Write to your Muse.

    Journal/write to your Muse for fifteen to thirty minutes every day. Ask your Muse to help you create a new story. It may not happen all at once ... stories unfold. Keep journaling and ask your Muse to guide you. Keep a Moleskine notebook in your pocket—you never know when the Muse will appear!

Benefit Three:
Connection at Work

Connection at Work
- Defines the meaning we attach to work
- Greater commitment and productivity

UNDERSTANDING THE VARIOUS WAYS WE ARE CONNECTED IN THE WORLD GIVES US A GREATER SENSE OF HOW AND WHY WE ARE CONNECTED IN OUR WORKPLACE. NOT ONLY ARE WE CONNECTED TO OTHER INDIVIDUALS, BUT WE ARE CONNECTED TO THE TYPE OF WORK WE DO, THE CULTURE, AND THE ENVIRONMENT.

To attach a greater meaning to our work enhances every aspect of our daily involvement in our workplace. Numerous studies have shown that people do not stay at jobs because of the money; they stay because of the meaning an individual attaches to the job or career. They stay because their job gives them a feeling of self-worth. Finding a place where we can integrate and feel connected to our work brings a different level of commitment and responsibility to whatever task we do.

Journaling heightens our awareness of what goes on around us and how we interact with our environment. Recently, a client told me that she wanted to change jobs. The money was great, but she felt no connection with the work or the environment. Her belief systems were not consistent with the projects that the business supported. She had little in common with the other people who worked at the business. As she journaled, she began to put her thoughts on paper and explore them. She identified her own belief systems. It was the clarity she needed to start to explore the workplace to find a business with which she could align and where her beliefs could be congruent with that of her employer. She could actually feel connected with the work and the part she played in the greater scheme of the company. This connection energized her work and brought greater fulfillment to her self and her new company.

Research has shown that writing forces people to stop and reevaluate their life circumstances. The cognitive changes allow individuals to begin to think about and use their social worlds differently. They talk more and connect with others differently. With these cognitive and social changes, many unhealthy behaviors decrease. As the studies have shown, expressive writing promotes sleep, enhanced immune function, and reduced alcohol consumption.

As you begin to journal through this next group of exercises and explore the deeper connections in your own personal life, allow for a parallel process to explore your work environment. This process will enable you to discover the meaning you attach to the work you do and the ripple effect your work creates in the world.

Exercises: Connection—Understanding and Experiencing Our Connection to All Things.

Sensory: Exploring the Senses

The right hemisphere of the brain holds the limbic system, which processes the independent streams of information that burst into our brain via the sensory system. We can all become caught in the emotional loops that run in our brain. Whether it is grief, loss, anger, joy, or any other emotion, the circuit will be triggered by the sensory system from the right brain.

Many of the clients whom I have seen in my practice have had a lot of loss. One of the stories I frequently hear is how difficult it is to go to the grocery store after a loved one has passed away. It was one of the most difficult things for me after the loss of my husband. I walked into the grocery store, started crying, and had to leave. Going to the grocery store is like a ritual for many families. I realized all of the things I no longer needed to buy. The sensory system gets highly activated by the sense of smell and the visuals surrounding you. Going to the grocery store activates our whole body.

Certain sounds, pictures, smells, and other information coming into us from the environment activate the sensory system. Become more aware of your sensory activation as you journal through the following questions.

1. *Close your eyes and ... Breathe, ... again, ... again, ... again!*

2. Describe a situation when you were "triggered" by your senses. What "old tape" did it bring up in your awareness? Describe.

3. Name the four people or animals in your life that you feel connected to. What connects you to each person or animal? Describe.

4. Name two to four places you feel connected to. What connects you to each place? Journal and describe those places.

5. Our sensory system is what makes us feel connected to everything else.

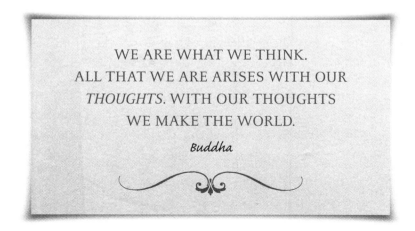

WE ARE WHAT WE THINK.
ALL THAT WE ARE ARISES WITH OUR
THOUGHTS. WITH OUR THOUGHTS
WE MAKE THE WORLD.

Buddha

Describe a time when you have felt connected to everything that existed.

Thoughts:

Thoughts are created as we move through the environment around us and our sensory system is activated. Thoughts are the most influential force we have in our lives. Thoughts repeated over and over become beliefs, and beliefs become habits. So, becoming aware of our thoughts is the first step in the process of becoming present. Our thoughts determine who we are and what we do in the world. Our actions follow our thoughts. Our thoughts are attached to emotions. Our inner thoughts can become our intentions, which is why we must monitor our thoughts.

A client recently told me a story about buying yogurt. She was standing at the checkout counter at the grocery store and realized with frustration that she had bought plain yogurt instead of the vanilla she had intended to buy. She started asking herself how she could make such a stupid mistake; how could she be so dumb! She was genuinely upset. This overreaction connected her thought immediately back to a childhood experience when her mother had chastised her for buying the wrong milk and paying ten cents too much for the milk. The yogurt incident activated her sensory system and the story she had stored about the milk.

Our thoughts build our stories from their attachment to certain neural pathways in our brain. As we learn to be aware of the thoughts in our head, we can learn to stop some of the negative tapes that seem to just "run." We have to be conscious of our thoughts in order to change them.

6. Listen to chatter in your head. For one day, try to monitor this chatter. When a negative thought or self-talk comes, think about what part of your sensory system is activated and what belief is attached to the thoughts. Write about what happens when you have a negative thought.

7. Write what the "truth" is about that thought pattern and the belief system that needs to change.

Emotions:

In Jill Bolte Taylor's book *My Stroke of Insight*, she describes how we respond to stimulation coming in through our sensory system during each day. Dr. Taylor says, "There are certain limbic system programs that can be triggered automatically, and it takes less than 90 seconds for one of these programs to be triggered, surge through our body, and then be completely flushed out of the blood stream."[23] She cites anger as one of the programmed responses that can be set off automatically. She says that once triggered, within ninety seconds from the initial trigger, the chemical component of anger has completely dissipated from the blood, and the automatic response is over. It is then, she says, that we have a choice either to hook back into the neurocircuitry or move back into the present moment, allowing the reaction to melt away.

8. Think about the experience that Taylor has described in the paragraph above. We all have emotions that get triggered automatically. It is important to acknowledge them and learn to manage them. Think of a situation that made you angry, close your eyes, and time yourself. See if you can let this situation run through your system for ninety seconds and move on to something else, a new thought—a present thought. If you cannot "let go" after ninety seconds, use this as information to explore this situation a little further by journaling/writing about it. Keep this exercise in your awareness and try it tomorrow when someone triggers something else in you. It is a great way to practice managing your emotions. It's a choice!

9. Cut a few pictures out of a magazine that attract you. Pick one picture out of the group of pictures. Look at the picture that you picked. Think about how this picture speaks to you.

Write about what meaning this picture holds for you, what thoughts it brings into your mind, and the emotions it brings up in you.

BELIEF SYSTEMS:

What you believe in your mind absolutely affects your biology and your actions. Once the subconscious mind accepts perceptions of something as "truth," it is hardwired into our own brains, becoming our "truth." Our thoughts create our truths. Consequently, programmed misconceptions in our subconscious mind are not "monitored" and can engage us in limited thinking and old, restrictive behaviors.

One of my belief systems when my husband died was that if you were not a stay-at-home mom, your children would simply not turn out right. My mother, sweet and well intentioned, had passed that belief on to me. When I went back to work after Tom's death and experienced a positive outcome from working, it rendered the old belief system that I had lived with seem completely incorrect. I then changed my thoughts to construct and support a new belief system that supported what I was doing and worked in my life.

When we have an experience, our response to the experience records a positive or negative outcome in our subconscious brain. The universe has a wonderful way of presenting situations to us again so that we can experience something in a new way. That sometimes requires us to change our belief systems. When we "let go" and allow ourselves to reexperience something in a new way, it helps us to change a belief system and move forward differently. It "heals" old wounds or beliefs and enables us to behave differently.

Here are a few examples of belief systems that I have encountered from clients who were stuck:

- My job is just to make money.
- If I do not get a certain grade or get into a specific school, I will be a failure.
- If I leave this job, I will never find another one.
- I could never make more than $_____ a year.
- I always fail at relationships.
- I am a terrible parent because_____.

- I am irresponsible because I am sometimes late.

10. Name a belief system (or more than one) that you have lived out of that might be judgmental to yourself or make you judge others. Journal/write about that.

11. What would happen if you changed that belief system?

12. What is a belief you have that might be released or changed to help you with an issue you cannot resolve? Journal/write about the issue and the belief system.

13. What is a belief that you might need to release or change for your path/story to unfold in a different way? Journal/write about that belief and how your story/life could change if you release that belief.

14. What is a belief system that has kept you from connecting with certain people or groups? How would your life or relationships change if that shifted or changed? (Example: I am not good enough to_____).

YOU HAVE A SILENT PARTNERSHIP WITH THE INFINITE. REST IN THIS DIVINE ASSURANCE AND THIS DIVINE SECURITY. THIS IS MORE THAN A SENTIMENT. KNOW THAT THE SPIRIT FLOWS IN TRANSCENDENT LOVELINESS INTO YOUR WORLD OF THOUGHT AND FORM, THAT IT FLOWS THROUGH YOUR WHOLE BEING, SPIRITUAL, EMOTIONAL, MENTAL AND PHYSICAL.

Ernest Holmes

Meditation and Spirituality:

As we explore connections, meditation and spirituality are the highest connection to everything that is possible. Without understanding and exploring our own personal connection to God, the Universe, or a Higher Power, we operate as a closed system. Journaling is a way to open our minds and become the observer of our lives in the context of the greater world and to explore at a deeper level what is our own understanding and relationship with God, the Universe, or Higher Power.

When I meditate, I go into a space of oneness with God. My breathing takes over, and I simply try to let my mind go blank. It is my time to listen. I usually try to write before or after I meditate. It is important for me to capture some thoughts before I go blank. It is sometimes helpful to write before you meditate, as it helps to download the "monkey mind" that seems to plague us when we become silent. Meditation helps me expand my consciousness and deepen my relationship with God.

Nature also helps me expand my understanding and relationship with God. No matter how separate things appear, nothing is separate when we immerse our minds into the field of everything that exists and connects around us.

Exercises:

15. When do you feel closest to God? Describe the time when you have that feeling.

16. Is there one incident that has drawn you closer to God, or pushed you away? Journal/write about what happened.

17. Are you in the process of defining or redefining your own spirituality? What has happened to make you want to do that? Write about what would help you to do that.

18. What do you need to change in your life to allow yourself to become closer to God/Spirit/Higher Power? Journal/write about what conscious actions you think you might be able to make to do that.

19. Pick a time when you can sit in nature, be silent, and write. Write about your connection to nature, describe the spot where you chose to write, and your connection to all things.

20. Write to your Muse: journal/write to your Muse for fifteen to thirty minutes or more each day. Spirituality is not meant to be separate from the body or mind. Ask your Muse how to integrate your awareness and experience of Spirit into every moment of your everyday life.

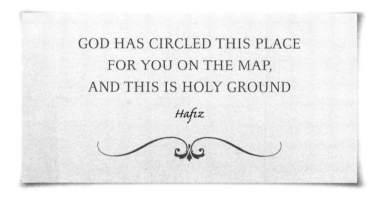

GOD HAS CIRCLED THIS PLACE
FOR YOU ON THE MAP,
AND THIS IS HOLY GROUND

Hafiz

Benefit Four:
Focus at Work

Focus at Work

- Improves clarity
- Increases focus
- Makes organization out of chaos

MOST WORK ENVIRONMENTS ARE BUSY PLACES! THERE IS USUALLY NOT A LOT OF TIME TO FOCUS ON ONE THING. OUR ENERGY CAN BE SCATTERED BY THE MULTITUDE OF TASKS AT HAND. IN ORDER TO BRING SOME ORDER TO THE CHAOS, WE HAVE TO UNDERSTAND WHAT A GREAT EFFECT JOURNALING CAN HAVE ON OUR ABILITY TO CONCENTRATE AND FOCUS.

Preoccupation is one of the biggest causes of people's inability to focus. Because so much of our time is spent focusing on the stories in our heads, it becomes frustrating as it distracts us from the tasks we need to complete. I hear story after story about people not being able to concentrate. When repetitive thoughts are running through our minds, it blocks new thoughts from activating. The most effective method to help relieve this preoccupation is to journal our thoughts for fifteen to twenty minutes at some point in the morning and again in the evening if possible. I have many clients who practice this faithfully and learn to stay calm amidst the chaos. As we clear our "monkey mind," new ideas can bubble up!

Studies show that the responses of individuals who are writing about emotional topics evidence immediate biological responses that are congruent with those seen among people attempting to relax.[24] In addition, behavioral changes have been found. Students who write about emotional topics evidence improvements in grades in the months following the study.[25]

Writing has also been shown to increase working memory.[26] After people write about troubling events, they devote less cognitive effort to them. This allows them to be better listeners, which would mean that they can absorb more information.

All of this data helps us to understand how journaling can help us to gain a sense of focus and concentration. Journaling is not a "quick fix." Our minds are actually not "quick" either, compared to a computer. So, journaling is a good fit for our minds. As you begin to answer the questions in this section, consider how this process will better equip you for the workplace. Better focus leads to greater clarity and productivity.

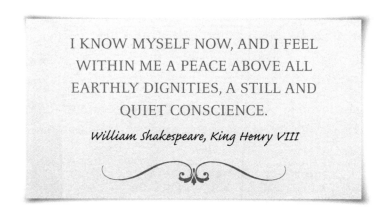

I KNOW MYSELF NOW, AND I FEEL
WITHIN ME A PEACE ABOVE ALL
EARTHLY DIGNITIES, A STILL AND
QUIET CONSCIENCE.

William Shakespeare, King Henry VIII

Exercises: Focus

MONKEY MIND:

My client Katie was a typical example of someone who had difficulty shutting down the thoughts that would not stop after a sudden loss. She had tried to return to work after being off for three days. She relayed her story of trying to return to work after the death of her daughter. She said that she almost had a wreck on the way to work. Her mind was still consumed with the details of every part of her daughter's recent death. It was as though her mind was grappling with trying to remember the details of the horrific last few weeks. She stated that throughout the day, she would find herself sitting at her desk and just staring at the computer screen. It was as if she was in a trance. She was thinking about all of the things that had happened when Mary was a little girl. She was retracing every part of her life. She was also very anxious and finding that everything that anyone said or did irritated her. Why was she even back here? Her whole body felt sick most of the time. Her boss was a very patient person, but he clearly did not understand the enormity of what she had been through. What could she do? She knew that she couldn't take off from work indefinitely. The conversation in her head would not end.

Whether we are stressed about work, or a relationship, or a sudden loss, we all feel that we should be able to return to normal after a crisis in our lives. The truth is, our sensory system is on overload. We cannot begin to process everything that has happened to us. Our body and mind are saying, "I need time. I am in shock." We need time to integrate all the pieces that are new information. What we knew as "truth" is no longer a part of our lives.

As you begin the exercises below, let your thoughts flow out onto the pages. It might take several days, or even weeks to regain focus. But, it will happen.

1. *Close your eyes and ... Breathe, ... again, ... again, ... again!*

2. What are the thoughts that are "running" through your mind at this moment? It might be several different situations, topics, subjects, or feelings. Whatever those thoughts are, take at least fifteen minutes,

and write down your thoughts now. Do this every morning and every evening, if possible. If morning does not work, use your coffee break at midmorning. See how much clearer and grounded you start to feel. You are creating a clear channel for new memory, new thoughts, and new focus.

INTENTION:

Our deepest intentions are carried not only in our minds but are felt throughout our bodies. Intentions are powerful, and the intention with which we do something is directly related to the result or outcome that we produce. For example, if I give money to a person or an organization to affect change or support some cause close to my heart, the money is being used for good. It is a very different intention if I give the money solely for my name to be used on something, or if I am just giving it so others will think I am a generous person. In the latter circumstances, the ego is controlling the intention. It can be a very positive thing for someone's name to be used on something, but it is all in the intention. When the ego is in control, it will not generate the same result for the person. It is important to think about your intention before taking an action. The more we focus on an intention, the more powerful it becomes.

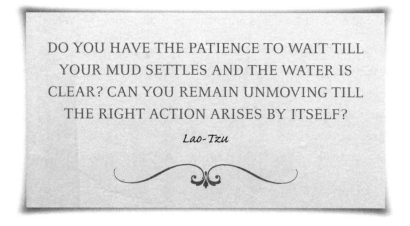

DO YOU HAVE THE PATIENCE TO WAIT TILL YOUR MUD SETTLES AND THE WATER IS CLEAR? CAN YOU REMAIN UNMOVING TILL THE RIGHT ACTION ARISES BY ITSELF?

Lao-Tzu

Some intentions are small and some are larger. As you set small intentions each day, you will feel your focus and energy start to shift as you have an inner knowing that as you go through your day, you are aligning yourself with a universal power in every action that you take. For example, if I set an intention to do the best job I can at work each day, I can focus my efforts knowing that my intention is supported by the universe, God, the quantum field, all responding to me, helping me to do this fantastic job. Think of the power in that intention! Intentions that are more complicated may take more time, as pieces may have to be put into place for that particular situation to manifest itself.

When an intention is written clearly, over and over, the solution starts to present itself as the mind is trained to focus on finding a solution. In Deepak Chopra's book *Ageless Body, Timeless Mind*, he states that "An intention is a signal sent from you to the field, and the result you get back from the field is the highest fulfillment that can be delivered to your particular nervous system."[27] Intention is one of the most powerful tools we have at our disposal. It is a conscious focus that starts a chain of events beginning in our brain with the reprogramming of our own neural pathways and connecting us with the greater quantum field. Repetition is an important part of reprogramming our brain, which is why writing our intentions over and over is important.

When writing an intention, it is important to think about the following things:

- Write the intention with clarity.
- Be specific about what you want, including as much detail as possible.
- Expect results.
- Keep track of your results.
- Think of other times in your life when you have gotten results.
- "Let go," knowing the highest fulfillment possible is in motion.

3. Write an intention now. Be as focused and detailed as possible.
4. Visualize and feel what it will be like when your intention manifests itself. Remember, your subconscious is programmed through your

sensory system. Close your eyes, and feel the sensations.

5. Rewrite your intention every day until you see results of some kind.

6. Journal/write about the results you got from your intention. If it was not the full result you wanted, search your mind for the block or barrier to that intention. Write about that.

7. Write a small intention each day. Example: I intend to be loving to everyone I meet today.

8. Journal/write what happens in response to the small intentions you write and set each day. You will be amazed at the opportunities that appear to support your small intention and the shifts that take place around you.

9. Write to your Muse:

    Journal/write to your Muse fifteen to thirty minutes each day. Ask your Muse for guidance to help you to be clear about what you want in your life and in describing your intentions. Write about what your life will be like when your intentions manifest themselves

Benefit Five:
Creativity at Work

Creativity at Work

- Enhances creativity
- Encourages conceptual thinking
- Diminishes "rote" thinking

MAKING OURSELVES OPEN TO THE CREATIVE FORCE WITHIN US REQUIRES THAT WE LEARN HOW TO EXPRESS OURSELVES—THROUGH WRITING, ART, PHOTOGRAPHY— WHATEVER WE CHOOSE. IT IS ONE THING TO UNDERSTAND OUR OWN CREATIVE GIFTS, BUT DETERMINING HOW TO USE OUR GIFTS IN THE WORK SETTING IS THE CHALLENGE.

Maggie was a wonderful employee for a real estate development company. She had come into my office to discuss her feelings about being limited in her job position. She was a sales assistant, really loved her company and did not want to leave, but felt that she had no passion for what she did. As she started to explore the exercises, she discovered that she wanted to expand her job beyond where she was, and she was feeling boxed in. After expanding her thinking and imagining what was "possible," she decided to talk to her boss about her ideas. He listened intently and was amazed at the creative concepts she had envisioned to expand her role. It would not only enhance her job but create a new line of business for the company. It was a win-win for everyone.

Creativity is expression. Studies show that writing our thoughts daily for fifteen to twenty minutes each day has enabled individuals to learn the art of expressing themselves simply and effectively. Such artistic expression requires awareness, and that awareness can be deepened through writing. As you learn to express and explore emotions by writing, that process can enhance the parallel artistic expression in your life.

Creativity is essential to the out-of–the-box skill set and conceptual thinking that is going to become even more important as businesses compete for the same services and dollars. As you journal through the questions on the pages pertaining to the benefit of creativity, ask yourself, "How can I encourage my artistic expression to come alive in me in my workplace?" No matter what your "job," there is a place for imagination and expression.

Exercises: Creativity

1. Close your eyes and ... Breathe, ... again, ... again, ... again!

2. When have you expanded yourself beyond what was ordinary or familiar? Write and describe that place.

3. How did that feel? Journal/write about that feeling.

4. What have you done in your life that feels the most natural to you; specifically, what calls you and makes you feel connected to your own rhythm, your own passion? Write and describe what that was and what it felt like.

5. Would you be willing to do that again? If yes, why? If no, why not?

6. What could you possibly change to allow you to explore that again? Explain.

7. How do you make yourself feel grounded? What does that feel like? Describe.

8. List some things that make you feel grounded.

9. When have you felt yourself in a "flow"? Journal/write about that time.

10. Start to observe the synchronicity in your life. Journal/write about those moments.

11. Make a plan for the next week. As you write your plan, include things in your plan that do the following:

    - Create silence, such as meditation or prayer.
    - Have one new experience, even if it is just driving to work a different way.
    - Spend some time outdoors, in nature.
    - Do one thing for yourself—yoga, an art class, Nia dance—where you can express yourself in a different way.
    - Make a creative object for someone you care about, a card, a picture.
    - Journal/write about how you feel in these new experiences.
    - Make a mandala.

12. Where is the place in your life where you express your creativity?

13. When have you had the opportunity to assimilate different pieces of your own life/career together and use them in new ways? Write about that.

14. Conceptual thinking is the ability to "see the big picture." When have you had that experience? In a career, personal life, relationship? Write about that.

INTUITION

Intuition is a matter of honoring the still, small voice inside of us that says, "Do this!" "Don't do that!" We can teach ourselves to use our intuition by being quiet and listening. It is hard to do that when cognitive reasoning is the voice that usually steers us around. Intuition is pure energy. When you receive an intuitive message, resist the urge to figure out what it means. Do not try to overdetermine the significance. Receive the information through the senses and just sit with it, knowing the outcome will be revealed to you. If you have an intuition that you absolutely should not do something, listen to that message.

15. When have you had an intuitive thought or received an intuitive message? Describe that situation.

16. The more you use your intuition, the more it will be available to you. This week, write each day about listening to your intuition, and what happened. As you test out your intuition, have fun with it!

IMAGINATION

I can remember lying in the front yard as a child, looking at the clouds, and making up stories in my head. That is exactly what imagination is, creating pictures in our minds out of images of all the possibilities we can imagine. Imagination has no limits. Every successful business or idea draws from someone's imaginative process.

As children, we daydream. As we get older and go through school, we have all heard the warning, "Stop daydreaming!" The reverse should actually be true. We should give awards for the best daydream. The great gift of imagination comes out of our conscious. To really explore the creative parts of ourselves, we have to enter the field of all possibility where our imagination can "play" with all the ideas that are not just possible, but impossible—the ideas that haven't been created yet. Allow your mind to create new neurons that explore your imagination. Enjoy!

17. When was the last time you daydreamed? Journal/write about your memory of that.

18. Schedule a time with yourself to let your imagination run free. Describe what you thought about. Don't feel guilty!

19. If you could imagine yourself doing anything, what would that be? Journal/write the details of that. Expand on this every day.

20. Think about what you wrote in the previous question. How do you see this fitting into the bigger picture of the world? Write about that.

21. Journal/write to your Muse: write to your Muse for fifteen to thirty minutes each day.

Ask your Muse to help you create a special place or time to explore your creative nature. Journal/write about how you might do that.

Benefit Six:
Authenticity at Work

Authenticity at Work

- Gives individuals a voice
- Increases level of integration and individual contribution

BRINGING ALL OF WHO YOU ARE INTO THE WORKPLACE IS IMPORTANT. BUT, IF YOU DON'T HAVE A GOOD GRASP OF WHO YOU ARE, ALL OF YOU, THAT PERSON DOESN'T REALLY SHOW UP. AS YOU BECOME THE OBSERVER OF YOUR LIFE THROUGH WRITING, YOU WILL BECOME MORE AND MORE AWARE OF THE PERSON YOU ARE BECOMING. AS YOU LET GO OF THE THINGS AND CLUTTER THAT DEFINE YOU, A NEW ENERGY WILL EMERGE. MANY TIMES WE WRITE DOWN OUR THOUGHTS AND IDEAS BEFORE WE ASSOCIATE A VOICE OR AN ACTION WITH THEM.

I met Frank several years ago. He was flying high—he thought he was a rock star; only he was really a broker. He lived the rock star life. He really wasn't sure who he was. Then, the market fell, Frank fell, and Frank's life came apart. His so-called friends, his wife, and his work colleagues no longer wanted anything to do with him because he "just couldn't keep up." This is an extreme example, but any of us can become Frank. To my surprise, Frank was in enough pain to try anything, so he began journaling. He wrote about who he had been as a young boy. He talked about the abuse he suffered, the pain he had gone through, and his reliance on drugs to numb the pain. The work he did became so obsessive that, for him, it was just another way to numb the feelings and stay on the endless treadmill. Meanwhile, he never stopped to think about the sad things that had happened to him in his life, and he remained afraid to look at who he really had become.

Journaling became Frank's way of taking apart his experiences and containing and looking at them in a way that didn't overwhelm him. When Frank went back to work, he chose a completely different field. He opted to do volunteer work with a nonprofit that ministered to young, delinquent boys. He eventually went on the board of the nonprofit and healed many of his own wounds through that work.

We change according to the experiences life brings us. As the layers are peeled back, your ability to be fully present at work will increase. Being present is one of the attributes of authenticity. Being fully present at work energizes not only yourself but your workplace and production.

As you delve into these authenticity exercises, you will explore and discover who you were created to be. This discovery will give you permission to have a voice and contribute more to yourself and your work.

Exercises: The Authentic Self

1. *Close your eyes and ... Breathe, ... again, ... again, ... again!*

2. What is the persona or personas of whom you think you "should" be? This could be cultural, family beliefs, etc. Journal/write about that persona or personas, and when you can let that persona go and when you cannot.

3. For one day, monitor yourself. Try being present in every situation you encounter. It takes a lot of work! Write about your experience of being

present and how different it feels.

4. As you allow yourself to "be yourself," what do you have to let go of? We have emotional clutter and physical clutter. What is the clutter in your life that keeps you stuck and that you need to let go of? (Clutter can be a title, stuff, way of life, or a barrier of any kind.) Write about that.

5. As you redesign your life, what are the components that make you feel resourceful and effective and reflect the person you are becoming?

Ego

Have you ever had the experience of looking back over a period in your life and said, "Who was that person!" A friend of mine was going through his boxes in his garage trying to decide what to keep and what to get rid of—probably something we can all relate to. As he looked through boxes of trophies and pictures of himself receiving awards, he said, "Who was that guy?" He had gone through a period in his life when he was completely out of balance and overidentified with his career and image in the community. His ego was fully in charge. He acknowledged that he probably really never "showed up," because when he did, it was all about his current title or the award. Fortunately, he could now clearly look back and see that person.

This is a great story about the ego. We need the ego to have an identity and define who we are in our lives. But, when the ego is "in charge," the balance shifts, and we confine ourselves to exist within the boxes the ego creates. The ego *loves* to be stroked, encourages separation, judges others, and always wants to have the answer—to be right.

Carl was a man who had gone to Harvard and was an executive with a large company. Carl wanted to support nonprofits in the world, so he decided to quit his executive position and started creating nonprofits in third-world countries. Fortunately for Carl, money was not the issue. All of a sudden, however, he didn't have a business card. He didn't have any of the titles or a place to go every day. Carl said that it was one of the hardest times in his life. At first, he felt depression, anxiety, and regret about his decision, based on a passion he had felt so drawn to. What happened? The ego went crazy! The ego sent the great message—you are worthless because you are no longer a ... name a category.

Slowly, Carl started to redefine his purpose and listen to the wisdom within to understand why he was so drawn to nonprofit work. As he went inward and became clear and defined about his purpose, everything started to change. Carl is one of the most authentic, energetic, and attractive people I know—who does incredible, amazing work in the small villages of the world.

It is important to think about our balance, and to monitor our ego. For example, when I give workshops, I have to monitor my ego. I have to remind myself that I am the messenger, and I am fortunate to be able to do this work in the world. It's not about me. If we can monitor the ego, we can use it to help us, not to control our actions and prevent us from becoming who we were created to be.

6. How has your ego affected you in the past? Journal/write about that person.

7. Think about when your ego affects you the most. Describe that person.

8. How can you become more aware of monitoring the ego?

9. Image yourself as a baby, before you had an ego. Think of all the gifts and potential that existed within this small child. Journal/write about who this child was created to be. This is a powerful exercise. Take your time writing this.

10. Journal/write to your Muse: write for fifteen to thirty minutes each day. For the next week, ask your Muse to point out when the ego is in control. Ask your Muse to help you become more aware of this. Write about when your ego was in charge this week. This may surprise you! Learn to laugh at your ego.

Benefit Seven:
Vision and Dreams at Work

Vision and Dreams at Work
- Improves boundaries
- Strengthens an organization by uniting the personal vision and the business vision

UNDERSTANDING YOUR PURPOSE IS IMPORTANT TO HELP ATTACH MEANING TO YOUR LIFE. YOUR PURPOSE IS USUALLY A COMMON THREAD THAT RUNS THROUGH THE VARIOUS ACTIVITIES, CAREERS, AND WAYS WE EXPRESS OURSELVES IN THE WORLD. OUR VISION MAY CHANGE, BUT THE PURPOSE WILL SHOW ITSELF THROUGH THE VISION. TYPICALLY, MANY OF OUR WAKING HOURS ARE SPENT AT WORK. AS WE STRIVE FOR BALANCE IN OUR LIVES, WRITING BECOMES A WAY TO HELP US GET A GLIMPSE OF THAT MEANING AS WE ARTICULATE OUR PASSION, PURPOSE, AND VISION TO ALIGN WITH WHERE WE SPEND MANY OF OUR WAKING HOURS—WORK.

After journaling through the other Six Benefits, the power of journaling should be evident. The writing defines your story and gives more clarity to your life. Your purpose and vision should emerge from the previously written pages. Your personal vision and business vision should compliment or reflect each other. As you align your visions, you will feel grounded and clear about what you have to contribute to your workplace.

When I returned to the workplace, I knew my simple purpose was to help others in some way to heal. I did this as a parent, then an employee at a family service center. As my career expanded, my purpose aligned with my vision, which continued to expand. That vision expanded and became "to enable every individual on the planet to heal," which then lead me into private practice, to a grief center for children, to become an author and write books about grief and loss, to work at a program at Baylor College of Medicine for children with chronic illness, and, finally, to author another book to help individuals look inside themselves to find their own wisdom, authenticity, and healing.

The vision of great men such as Andrew Carnegie, Bill Gates, and John Kennedy make us understand the power of not just reaching for the possible but reaching for the impossible.

As we formulate our thoughts to realize our vision and dreams, we grasp the enormous potential of what is available to us from our magnificent brains. As we draw on the new scientific information regarding neuroplasticity, we realize the unlimited ability to create new neural pathways, which wire these new thoughts and ideas together. According to scientists, this is only the tip of the iceberg.

The exercises in Benefit Seven will explore vision and dreams. As you integrate where you have been, what you have now, and where you are going, your life will become more manageable and a reflection of whom you were created to be.

Exercises: Vision and Dreams

1. *Close your eyes and ... Breathe, ... again, ... again, ... again!*

2. Journal/write about any preoccupation that is repeating itself in your mind.

Write about it every day for fifteen to thirty minutes to help clear the repetitive thoughts. This may take several days every week for a while.

3. Journal about how you would like your life to be. As you redefine yourself, include the following:
   - Where you would like to live (mountains, city, etc.)
   - The lifestyle you would like to have (travel, exercise, etc.)
   - The type of work you would like to have and the schedule
   - The people you would like to be with
   - Identify your passion! (You may have already done this in the Creativity section)
   - Define your purpose or some components of what that might be
   - Spiritual beliefs
   - Financial goals

   Journal/write about this as if it were happening now. Create a vivid, written picture.

4. Think of another time in your life when you were really happy, joyful, and passionate. Include the skills you mastered at that time and all aspects of the situation. Feel it throughout your body. Write about this time.

5. Focus on one aspect of what you wrote in question 3 that you do not currently have in your life. Identify all the parts of that. For example, the type of work. Journal and describe in detail what you want that part of your life to look like. Repetition is the key. Write about this every day.

6. Visualize what having that "one thing" would feel like. This should be similar to the feeling you had in question 4. Do this several times a day along with your journaling. Write about the key concepts of this part of your vision. Keep them on a piece of paper and keep them with you. Focus on them every day.

7. Create a poster that reflects your new lifestyle. Keep it where you can see it and look at it every day.

PURPOSE:

This question seems to be on everyone's mind these days. What is your "purpose" on the planet? Purpose does not have to be complicated; it can be as simple as "helping others." It is important to identify our purpose in order to have a vision that fits our purpose. The following is an exercise that has proven useful to many who are trying to define their purpose.

8. Make a list of everything you have done in your life. Work, home, relationships, family, church activities, social activities—all of it. After you list all the things you have done, look for the common thread that runs through each thing. There is always a thread. You just have to find it. It will show itself to you. When you find the thread, write down the words that describe it. That is your purpose. Your purpose can manifest itself in many ways. Your vision may change throughout your life; your purpose will not. Write about the various ways your purpose has manifested itself in your life.

VISION:

Vision statements vary at different times in your life. Some of my clients have gotten stuck thinking that what they write will never be able to change. A vision statement does not have to be complicated. If you are writing a personal vision statement, it may include your purpose and the way you want to affect people's lives at this time. The same is true with a business. As a business grows, the vision will change as it expands.

A vision statement is a broad statement that should include the following:

- Your purpose and passion;
- Your concept of how you are going to express that vision in the world.
- The statement should be short, only a few sentences.
- It should be written in the now, not in the future.

9. Journal/write about everything you would like to include in your vision statement. Include your purpose in your vision.

Example: My purpose is to help others find joy. Vision: my vision is to help others find joy by taking beautiful pictures for everyone in the world to see.

10. Write a personal vision statement for yourself. Your personal vision should include things you are passionate about and what you think your purpose is on the planet. Keep this statement with you, in your pocket. Carry it around. Put it in your office, or on your computer, where you can see it. It will guide everything in your life toward your vision.

11. Identify some small steps you can take toward realizing your vision.

12. Make a vision board with pictures that reflect your vision.

13. Write to your Muse: journal/write to your Muse fifteen to thirty minutes each day. Write a question to your Muse before you go to bed about something you are not clear about in your future. Ask your Muse to provide the answer. Keep your journal beside your bed in case the answer comes in the form of a dream.

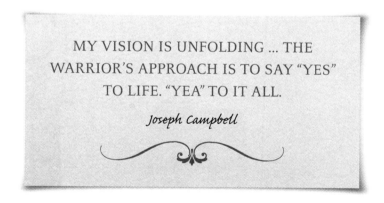

MY VISION IS UNFOLDING ... THE WARRIOR'S APPROACH IS TO SAY "YES" TO LIFE. "YEA" TO IT ALL.

Joseph Campbell

Additional Questions for Insight:
AT WORK:

14. Write a vision for your business. If you work within a business, write what your vision is for yourself during the time you are working in that business. It should support your personal business vision as well as the

business vision of the company. Journal before you write the vision.

15. Look carefully at your personal vision and your business vision. If your purpose is clear in both, your personal vision and your business vision should compliment each other.

16. What does success feel like to you? Describe that in detail. Write this in the present tense.

17. Write the small steps you could begin to take in order to go toward your vision.

PART FOUR

Tools for Transforming
Your Life

*T*HIS SECTION IS INTENDED TO HELP YOU EXTEND AND SUPPORT THE WORK YOU ARE DOING AS YOU PEEL BACK THE LAYERS TO FIND YOUR WISDOM WITHIN. IT INCLUDES THE FOLLOWING TOOLS:

- *Rewriting the Story:* A template to support you in separating situations into manageable pieces, so it does not feel so overwhelming as you rewrite your story.
- *Rehearsal:* This is a process that provides a structure to implement your Vision and Dreams.
- Worksheet templates for goal setting.
- Meditation to set the stage for the quiet stillness you can use to enhance the journaling process.

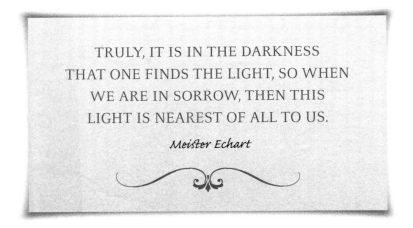

TRULY, IT IS IN THE DARKNESS
THAT ONE FINDS THE LIGHT, SO WHEN
WE ARE IN SORROW, THEN THIS
LIGHT IS NEAREST OF ALL TO US.

Meister Echart

Rewriting the Story

One of the first books I wrote was a guided journal on loss. As I wrote that journal, I realized that every situation involves a process that we must go through to get to the next step. I have put together a template to assist individuals in journaling through any situation. This template is intended to be a source for you to go to when you experience a difficult situation along your path.

It is important to understand that every situation we are dealing with involves varied elements of emotion and learning. Some situations take longer than others to process, depending upon the severity of the situation. When I was grappling with the death of my husband, Tom, it took me years to focus on the transformational part of the grief and loss process, which is included in the following model.

This template is a guide to help you through the various stages each individual must go through in order to process a situation in their lives. If we hurry the process, we simply will not heal the wounds or understand the lessons the situation has to teach us. Lessons reveal themselves over time. Be mindful of your own process as you begin your journey through one of life's transgressions.

Events or situations in our lives can feel unmanageable until they are broken down into manageable pieces, enabling us to step back and process the various parts. As our words ripple onto the pages, it gives us the opportunity to become the observer, to sort through our own "truth," allowing us to release the thoughts that hold us captive. The containment offered in each section of the template gives us a way to continue the gentle forward movement that journaling provides.

I have used this template with clients and in workshops. It helps to keep us from getting stuck in a situation and leads us to the "next step." As you continue to "rewrite" your own story, may this template help you to know that we are in a never-ending process of healing, alignment, and transformation, and, as we peel back the layers, that there is always a "next step."

Template for Journaling Through Any Situation

IDENTIFICATION OF THE SITUATION:

The first step toward the resolution of a problem or situation is to clarify the situation. Sometimes we minimize problems or are in denial that a situation exists. We cannot change anything until we understand what we are actually dealing with. As we identify the situation, we can become aware of the enormous range of feelings that it is triggering. We must acknowledge the changes this situation has caused in our lives and the effects on our physical, emotional, and spiritual bodies. By identifying the situation, you can give attention to your own thoughts, emotions, and actions surrounding that specific situation and how it is affecting your life at the moment.

1. Identify your situation, such as loss of a loved one, finances, relationship, addiction, etc.
2. What are the emotions, thoughts, and behaviors this situation triggers?
3. What are the changes that have come about in my life because of this situation?

INTEGRATION AND REFORMATION OF THE SITUATION:
Recognition and acceptance of where you are now is essential to understand how you can integrate this lesson into your life in order to enable you to move forward toward the next step. Begin the process by examining the beliefs that possibly limit your ability to grow from this experience and the wounds this situation is challenging you to explore in yourself. This is the opportunity to look at your life as it is now, determining how it has changed because of this situation, and how to respond to your new environment. Write an alternative course of action that could help this situation. In this stage, we are committing ourselves to a new relationship with our self and the Divine, exploring what the next steps are to move forward.

1. What beliefs or behaviors is this situation challenging me to explore in myself?
2. How has my life changed in relation to my environment, my relationships, and my spirituality?
3. What are some of the small steps I can take to respond to my new environment?

RECONSTRUCTION/METAMORPHOSIS/TRANSFORMATION OF THE PROCESS OR SITUATION.

Try to understand how this situation or experience might be used as a tool to change some of your beliefs, thoughts, emotions, behaviors, and actions. Instead of resistance, accept the situation as a vehicle to develop the undeveloped parts of your self. Finding meaning in difficult situations awakens us to the process of becoming alive again. How could this situation be perceived differently and change the story—and the outcome? Allowing yourself to be responsible for your life opens you to a new level of consciousness, which joins with the transformational power of the mystical presence of God.

1. What has shifted in my beliefs, or perceptions, or consciousness as a result of this situation?
2. How will my life be different going forward because of this situation?
3. How have my spirituality and my way of being in the world changed because of my situation?

Rehearsal

A DAILY PRACTICE TO CONNECT MY VISION AND DREAMS AND PUT THEM INTO ACTION.

Rehearsal is a process that has been created and used by a friend of mine. He has been extremely successful in the business world and has used this daily for many years. The act of doing the rehearsal not only sets intentions for the day, but the repetition actually sets a "play" in motion that allows the participant to be a part of the play. That is why he called this exercise "rehearsal." As you become a participant in your own vision and dreams, it allows the play to unfold.

1. Journaling/looking at the world from eighteen thousand feet. Most people are living from moment to moment and never take the time to step back and really look at how they are spending their time. Looking at the world from eighteen thousand feet helps us to step back from ourselves and see the big picture. Picture yourself looking down on

your life journey. What do you see? What do you see going forward? Journal/write about this big picture. This needs to be done at a break point such as the beginning of a new year. It can be done in the form of goal setting.

2. Write down your personal vision and your professional vision. Break them out according to your priorities and number them relative to their priority. Make a list of yearly goals from these priorities.

3. Now, break down the priorities into steps that can become monthly goals for the coming year. Identifying these monthly steps or goals will help you move toward achieving your yearly goals.

4. As you look at the monthly goals, identify the steps you can incorporate each week, keeping in mind their priority relative to what you have set at the beginning of the year.

5. At the beginning of each week, set your calendar for the days of that week, always keeping these yearly goals in mind and their priority. Keeping the yearly goals somewhere in front of you is important.

6. At the beginning of each day of the week, as mentioned in the above exercise, take the time to rehearse that day's goals, always keeping in mind how they fit the yearly goals. Keep in mind that you need to write/journal each day as well. This helps the process to stay clear.

- Create a list of all the things you need to do for the week.
- Break the list into days.
- Remove everything from the list that does not have anything to do with your visions.
- Rehearse what is going to happen today in the morning before leaving your home.
- The power of rehearsal, and reviewing what you are doing each day, is that everything that does not pertain to one of your goals or priorities drops off the radar.
- Keep in mind the list may change as you go through the year relative to priorities; that is okay.

- Don't be too hard on yourself.
- You will find that you will make huge progress toward fulfilling your personal and professional visions.
- You will end up with a lot of free time that you didn't have before!

Worksheet 1

MY PERSONAL VISION:

_____

_____

_____

_____

_____

_____

_____

_____

_____

_____

_____

_____

_____

MY PROFESSIONAL VISION:

_____

_____

_____

_____

_____

_____

_____

_____

_____

_____

_____

_____

Worksheet 2

PRIORITIES FROM MY PERSONAL VISION:

_____

_____

_____

_____

_____

_____

BIG YEARLY GOALS:

_____

_____

_____

_____

_____

_____

PRIORITITES FROM MY PROFESSIONAL VISION:

_____

_____

_____

_____

_____

_____

BIG YEARLY GOALS:

_____

_____

_____

_____

_____

_____

Worksheet 3

MONTHLY GOALS:
JANUARY Priority/Goal

_____

_____

_____

_____

_____

_____

FEBRUARY Priority/Goal

_____

_____

_____

_____

_____

_____

MARCH **Priority/Goal**

_____

_____

_____

_____

_____

_____

APRIL **Priority/Goal**

_____

_____

_____

_____

_____

_____

MAY Priority/Goal

_____

_____

_____

_____

_____

_____

JUNE Priority/Goal

_____

_____

_____

_____

_____

_____

JULY Priority/Goal

_____

_____

_____

_____

_____

_____

AUGUST Priority/Goal

_____

_____

_____

_____

_____

_____

SEPTEMBER Priority/Goal

_____

_____

_____

_____

_____

_____

OCTOBER Priority/Goal

_____

_____

_____

_____

_____

_____

NOVEMBER Priority/Goal

_____

_____

_____

_____

_____

_____

DECEMBER Priority/Goal

_____

_____

_____

_____

_____

_____

Worksheet 4

Week: _____

Weekday: _____

Priority/Goals:

_____

_____

_____

_____

_____

_____

_____

_____

Things to do list:

1. *Journal/review your vision.*

2.

3.

4.

5.

6.

7.

8.

9.

10.

- Remove everything from the list that does not have anything to do with your vision.
- Rehearse what is going to happen today.

Meditation

The emergence into a still place is the call of meditation.
As you go inward and the silence surrounds you,
allow your mind to become still.
When thoughts emerge and try to pull you
away from the silence, it may help to focus on a mantra—
one word that reflects your spiritual belief.
Allow your self to connect with the Divine ...
listen to the whisper ... listen again ... and again ...

As you breathe, connect with the breath of the Divine ...
He is listening ... breathing in unison with you ...

The following meditations were written to help you sink into that
deeper place ... into a Oneness with the Divine.

By Angela Caughlin

A Meditation—
Through the Mystical Bliss

There is a field surrounding me. I am starting to remember ... I came into the planet in the middle of an energetic, mystical field called Bliss ... It appears white, with silver and gold threads running throughout, and dots that twinkle like little lights, swirling and surrounding my physical body. It surrounded me at birth, when I entered the planet. I can feel the energy when I am still. It hums like a vibration ... It moves with me. The more I think about Bliss, the more powerful it becomes; hundreds of tiny atoms and molecules that move with me, and surround my body. My physical body is in the middle of this mystical field and is constantly absorbing this Bliss ... giving me energy, health, guidance, new cells, and my energetic demeanor. This Bliss is surrounding and moving with me at all times ... bringing me new thoughts and ideas ... and leading me to new experiences ... I can trust my Bliss field ... it is constantly regenerating every atom and molecule, as it connects me to my past and my future ...

My mystical Bliss body is like the music of nature ... it is part of a symphony that has been there forever. Fire cannot burn it. Water cannot wet it. Wind cannot dry it. It was never born, and it never dies. I no longer have to be a victim to the conditional thoughts of my past, because I now see the world through the eyes of the Bliss that surrounds me. As Bliss becomes alive in me, it is as if I am seeing the world for the first time. With each breath, I am now absorbing my Bliss, my sheer unbounded joy and awareness of immortality. I am no longer my prior experiences, my past. My new awareness has sparked and connected me to my energetic field called Bliss ... this is the universe moving and communicating with me ... pulsating, surrounding, and holding my body, my thoughts, as Bliss is becoming a part of me and the essence of who I am ... I am no longer afraid ... I have crossed the threshold, knowing that as my awareness of my energy field grows, my experiences in the world will no longer be the same. Mystical Bliss is my immortality that will guide me through the rest of my life and beyond ...

By Angela Caughlin

My Imaginary
with the Divine

Close your eyes and put your hand on your heart. Feel your breath. The breath connects us with God, Oneness, the Divine.

Take another deep breath. Imagine that you are breathing in the breath of God, the Creator, the Divine. Feel your spirit absorbing the energy of this breath. Feel the breath guiding your spirit back to its true nature, the soul.

Breathe deeply again ...

As you breathe, feel your spirit and soul aligning with the power of this new breath and energy within you. As you return to Oneness, your soul is being restored.

During the day, whenever you breathe, think about the connections, think about it, repeat the words ... and recall the picture ... and breathe ... Oneness.

By Angela Caughlin

Visualization
for "The Path"

Close your eyes. A cobblestone path appears before you. The rocks are smooth and cool. You take off your shoes to feel the cool, smooth rocks underneath your feet. As you walk down the path you gaze around ... There are beautiful trees and flowers all around on either side of the path and a sparkling blue sky above. The flowers are vibrant colors of yellow, red, blue, and purple. As you continue down the path, you hear the sound of trickling water. The sound grows stronger. You see a stream of water starting to gently flow over the rocks in the stream. You are drawn to stop and watch the trickling water over the rocks. You draw closer and sit on a large, smooth rock beside the stream. You dangle your bare feet in the cool water. The water feels cleansing. You take a deep breath. As you breathe in, you look up and see a rainbow. You look at the beautiful colors in the rainbow and start to breathe in the colors, one at a time. First red, reminding you of courage, you breathe in the color deep down inside of you. Exhale ... Yellow, reminding you of joy, you breathe the color deep into your stomach. You feel joy. Exhale ... Then blue, breathe in calm and cool blue, inhaling the color deep inside all parts of you. Exhale ... Now breathe in green, deep inside of you. cleansing all parts of you. Exhale ... Now breathe purple, the color of spiritual knowledge, deep into all parts of your body. Gently exhale ... And now, breathe pink, the color of love ... through all of your body and into your heart. Exhale ... Breathe again ... knowing all of the colors have become a part of you and your body ...

At the end of the rainbow, you see a pot of gold. Its brilliant, yellow, golden light shimmers in the distance, casting yellow and silver magical threads. The light becomes stronger and stronger and connects with your energy, your being, as it seems to wrap around you, beckoning you. You breathe in the shimmering light. This light represents clarity, love, wisdom, guidance, and cleansing. You breathe in the golden, shimmering light again, all the way down through your body. Your body is filled with this new light. You continue to breathe, filling your body with this new light, this new energy. With a renewed sense of security and clarity, you step back on the cobblestone path, knowing that you have received a great gift. As you leave the beautiful garden, you know that each time you return, the garden and its energy will guide you where you need to go.

By Angela Caughlin

— *Notes* —

INTRODUCTION
[1] Frankl, *Man's Search for Meaning.*

PART ONE
[2] Gelb, *Think Like Leonardo da Vinci.*

[3] Lipton, *Biology of Belief.*

[4] Assaraf and Smith, *The Answer.*

[5] Pert, *Molecules of Emotion.*

[6] Chopra, *Ageless Body, Timeless Mind.*

[7] McFadden, "Synchronous Firing."

[8] Petrie et al., "Disclosure of Trauma."

[9] Francis and Pennebaker, "Putting Stress into Words."

[10] Spera, Buhrfeind, and Pennebaker, "Expressive Writing."

[11] See note 8 above.

[12] Pennebaker, Colder, and Sharp, "Accelerating the Coping Process."

[13] Boals and Klein, "Word Use."

[14] Boals and Klein, "Expressive Writing"; Boals and Klein, "Relationship of Life Stress."

PART TWO

[15] Taylor, *My Stroke of Insight.*

[16] Chopra, *Ageless Body, Timeless Mind.*

PART THREE

[17] Pennebaker and Susman, "Disclosure of Traumas."

[18] Pennebaker and Beall, "Confronting a Traumatic Event."

[19] Francis and Pennebaker, "Putting Stress into Words;" and Spera, Buhrfeind, and Pennebaker, "Expressive Writing."

[20] Francis and Pennebaker, "Putting Stress into Words."

[21] Pennebaker, Colder, and Sharp, "Accelerating the Coping Process."

[22] Pennebaker, "Writing about Emotional Experiences"; and Pennebaker and Susman, "Disclosure of Traumas."

[23] Taylor, *My Stroke of Insight.*

[24] Pennebaker, Hughes, and O'Huron, "The Psychophysiology of Confession."

[25] Lumley and Provenzano, "Stress Management through Written."

[26] Boals and Klein, "Expressive Writing"; and Boals and Klein, "Relationship of Life Stress."

[27] Chopra, *Ageless Body, Timeless Mind.*

— *Bibliography* —

Amen, Daniel G. *Change Your Brain, Change Your Life*. New York: Three Rivers Press, 1998.

Assaraf, John, and Murray Smith. *The Answer*. New York: Atria Books, 2008.

Baikie, Karen A., and Kay Wilhelm. "Emotional and Physical Health Benefits of Expressive Writing." *Advances in Psychiatric Treatment* 11 (2005): 338–46.

Boals, Adriel, and Kitty Klein. "Cognitive-Emotional Distinctiveness: Separating Emotions from Non-Emotions in the Representation of a Stressful Memory." *Memory* 13 (2005): 638–48.

———. "Expressive Writing Can Increase Working Memory Capacity." *Journal of Experimental Psychology: General* 130 (2001): 520–33.

———. "The Relationship of Life Stress and Working Memory." *Applied Cognitive Psychology* 15 (2001): 565–79.

———. "Word Use in Emotional Narratives about Failed Romantic Relationships and Subsequent Mental Health." *Journal of Language and Social Psychology* 24 (2005): 252–68.

Borysenko, Joan. *Fire in the Soul: A New Psychology of Spiritual Optimism*. New York: Warner Books, 1993.

Bradbury, Ray. *Zen in the Art of Writing: Essays on Creativity*. Santa Barbara, CA: Capra Press, 1990.

Bruce, Ray. "Strange But True: Improve Your Health through Journaling." *SelfhelpMagazine*, May 28, 1998. http://www.selfhelpmagazine.com/articles/health/journal.html.

Cameron, Julia. *The Complete Artist's Way: Creativity as a Spiritual Practice*. New York: Penguin Group, 2007.

Chopra, Deepak. *Ageless Body, Timeless Mind: The Quantum Alternative to Growing Old*. New York: Harmony Books, 1993.

———. *Quantum Healing: Exploring the Frontiers of Mind/Body Medicine*. New York: Random House, 1990.

Chopra, Deepak, and David Simon. *Grow Younger, Live Longer: 10 Steps to Reverse Aging*. New York: Three Rivers Press, 2001.

Create Write Now. "Is the Pen Mightier than the Pill?" Fall 1999. http://createwritenow.com/resources.html.

Davis, Braden. "Writing for Your Life." The Integrated Learning Center, Arizona State University. http://www.ilc.arizona.edu/johnson/classes/EDP512/Davis/paper.html.

Davis, Margie. "Writing to Heal." MedicineNet.com. http://www.medicinenet.com/script/main/art.asp?articlekey=53961 (accessed September 12, 2007).

Diamond, John. "How Thoughts Make You Weak." Lynne McTaggart Blog, November 9, 2007. http://livingthefield.ning.com/profiles/blogs/866644:BlogPost:29890.

Francis, M.E., and J.W. Pennebaker. "Putting Stress into Words: The Impact of Writing on Psychological, Absentee, and Self-Reported Emotional Well-Being Measures." *American Journal of Health Promotion* 6 (1992): 280–87.

Frankl, Victor E. *Man's Search For Meaning*. Rev. ed. New York: Washington Square Press, 1984.

Futrelle, David. "The Big Tease." *Fast Company*, December 2007, 43–52.

Gelb, Michael J. *How to Think Like Leonardo da Vinci: Seven Steps to Genius Every Day*. New York: Bantam Dell, 2004.

Levy, Steven. "The Future of Reading." *Newsweek*, November 26, 2007, 57–64.

Linden, David E. J., Ulrich Kallenbach, Armin Heineckeo, Wolf Singer, and Rainer Goebel. "The Myth of Upright Vision: A Psychological and Functional Imaging Study of Adaptation to Inverting Spectacles." *Perception* 2 (1999): 469–81.

Lipton, Bruce H. *The Biology of Belief: Unleashing the Power of Consciousness, Matter and Miracles*. Santa Rosa, CA: Mountain of Love/Elite Books, 2005.

Lumley, M.A. and K.M Provesano. "Stress Management through Written Emotional Disclosure Improves Academic Performance among College Students with Physical Symptoms." *Journal of Educational Psychology* 95 (2003): 641-649

McFadden, Johnjoe. "Synchronous Firing and Its Influence on the Brain's

Electromagnetic Field Theory of Consciousness." *Journal of Consciousness Studies*, May 2002.

McTaggart, Lynne. *The Field: The Quest for the Secret Force of the Universe.* Rev. ed. New York: Harper, 2008.

Miranda, C. *Stress Management Technique.* http://www.add-adhd-helpcenter. com/stress/stress_management_technique.html (accessed October 22, 2006).

NoHoArtsDistrict.com. "Writing for the Artist as Therapy." http://www. nohoartsdistrict.com/literary_arts/how_to_writing_therapy.htm (accessed December 5, 2007).

Parker-Pope, Tara. "The Power of Words for Cancer Patients." *New York Times*, February 26, 2008, National edition, Health section, Well Blog.

Pennebaker, James W. *Opening Up: The Healing Power of Expressing Emotions.* Rev. ed. New York: Guilford Press, 1997.

———. "Writing about Emotional Experiences as a Therapeutic Process." *Psychological Science* 8, no. 3 (1997): 162–66.

Pennebaker, J. W., and S. Beall. "Confronting a Traumatic Event: Toward an Understanding of Inhibition and Disease." *Journal of Abnormal Psychology* 95 (1986): 274–81.

Pennebaker, James W., and Cindy K. Chung. "Expressive Writing, Emotional Upheavals, and Health." In *Handbook of Health Psychology*, edited by H. Friedman and R. Silver, 263– 84. New York: Oxford University Press, 2007.

Pennebaker, J. W., M. Colder, and L. K. Sharp. "Accelerating the Coping Process." *Journal of Personality and Social Psychology* 58 (1990): 528–37.

Pennebaker, J. W., C. F. Hughes, and R. C. O'Huron. "The Psychophysiology of Confession: Linking Inhibitory and Psychosomatic Processes." *Journal of Personality and Social Psychology* 52 (1987): 781–79.

Pennebaker, J. W., and J. R. Susman. "Disclosure of Traumas and Psychosomatic Processes." *Social Science and Medicine* 26 (1988): 327–332.

Perez-Pena, R. "Success Without Ads: Consumer Reports Thrives on Subscriptions Only, Even on the Web." *New York Times*, December 8, 2007, sec. B.

Pert, Candace B. *Molecules of Emotion: The Science Behind Mind-Body Medicine.*

New York: Touchstone, 1999.

Petrie, K. J., R. Booth, J. W. Pennebaker, K. P Davison, and M. Thomas. "Disclosure of Trauma and Immune Response to Hepatitus B Vaccination Program." *Journal of Consulting and Clinical Psychology* 63 (1995): 787–792.

Pink, Daniel H. *A Whole New Mind: Why Right-Brainers Will Rule the Future.* New York: Riverhead Books, 2006.

Porterfield, K. "Journaling the Cancer Journey." http://www.kporterfield.com/journal/Cancer_Journey.html (accessed December 17, 2007).

———. "Keeping a Journal When Words Fail." http://www.kporterfield.com/journal/visual_grief.html (accessed December 5, 2007).

———. "Keeping a Nature Journal." http://www.kporterfield.com/journal/Journal_Nature.html (accessed December 5, 2007).

———. "Spark Your Creativity with a Dream Journal." http://www.kporterfield.com/creativity/Dream_Journal.html (accessed December 5, 2007).

———. "Speaking Topics: Discover the Power of the Pen." http://www.kporterfield.com/about_me/Journal_Topics.html.

Purcell, M. "The Health Benefits of Journaling." PsychCentral, December 12, 2006. http://psychcentral.com/lib/2006/the-health-benefits-of-journaling/.

Salter, Chuck. "Girl Power." *Fast Company*, December 19, 2007, 104–112.

Scherer, John J. *Five Questions That Change Everything Life: Lessons at Work.* Fort Collins, CO: Word Keepers, 2009.

Snyder, C. "Daily Power Words: The Healing Powers of Journaling." http://dailypowerwords.com/journaling.html (accessed January 28, 2006).

Spera, Stephanie P., Eric D. Buhrfeind, and James W. Pennebaker. "Expressive Writing and Coping with Job Loss." *Academy of Management Journal* 27, no. 3 (1994): 722–33.

Stratton, George M. "Some Preliminary Experiments on Vision without Inversion of the Retinal Image." *The Psychological Review* 3 (1896): 611–17.

Taylor, Jill Bolte. *My Stroke of Insight: A Brain Scientist's Personal Journey.* New York: Viking, 2008.

Ullrich, Philip M., and Susan K. Lutgendorf. "Journaling About Stressful Events: Effects of Cognitive Processing and Emotional Expression." *Annals of Behavioral Medicine* 24 (2002): 244–50.

The University of Auckland."Emotional Writing Improves HIV Patients." March 25, 2004. http://www.auckland.ac.nz/uoa/.

The University of Texas M.D. Anderson Cancer Center. "Writing for Wellness: Keeping a Journal." *OncoLog* 52, no. 4/5 (2007): 1–3.

Wexler, Mark. E-mail message to Angela Caughlin, February 26, 2009. Wexler explained the references to the "NASA experiment" on inverted vision. Laboratoire Psychologie de la Perception, Paris, France. http://wexler.free.fr.

Woolston, C. "Writing for Therapy Helps Erase Effects of Trauma." CNN.com, March 16, 2000.http://archives.cnn.com/2000/HEALTH/03/16/health.writing. wmd/ (accessed December 5, 2007).

— Acknowledgments —

*T*his book is the product of hundreds of clients who, over the past eighteen years, have taught me the difficult questions that must be asked. These are questions that help us to reach inside to access the wisdom that helps us examine and direct our own paths. For them I am grateful.

I am also grateful for the many workshop participants and their lively discussions that helped me put the questions in a format that has become the workbook that it is today. These participants and my clients believed enough in the process of journaling to try it, enabling me to continue to see the amazing results of this simple act and to continue to pursue the question of *why*.

This book would not have come into existence, however, without a wonderful group of support people on my path. It is my unseen team that has supported me from behind the scenes—at all times of the day and night. I wish to give thanks to them: to Mary Jo Langston, who, without our long evening walks, I just would not have made it; to all of my fellow practitioners at Spectrum Center and for the inspiration they continually bring into my life; to Kathy Davis, Barbara Malone, Meg Lauck, Holly Davis, Patricia Tyler, Melissa Rayburn, Jeni Halliday, Kathleen Murray, Lisa Osten, Mary Sue Rabe, and Merrill Lewen, who have all held my vision and watched it grow; and to Kathy Filippone, for her long hours spent on finding exactly the right titles for the research I was looking for.

I also wish to thank my publisher, Bright Sky Press—Rue Judd, Ellen Cregan, and Lucy Chambers, who have helped me birth this work into the world. What an amazing team of women! And my brilliant, patient editor, Hillary Durgin Harmon, who knows so much more than me that I know I am in good hands. I don't know how I got so lucky.

My family has been a major influence in writing this book. My mother, Mary Jane, always encouraged me to write in my diary and totally respected my privacy—that was the beginning. Special thanks to my sister, Mary, who has been an example of quiet constant support, and my brother, John, who has read and reread pages with unending patience.

Nothing would have happened without my children, Kelly, Melissa, and Tom, who encouraged me to pursue my own dreams and who are the most amazing, authentic people I know. I am very proud of each of them as I watch them carve out their own paths in the world. And last, but certainly not least, I am grateful to my best friend, coach, and partner, Bubba Levy, who patiently supported me through the process of writing and listened to endless rewrites along the way.

I have learned from everyone whom I have mentioned and am so grateful for the many teachers and experiences that have led me on this path.